MY WHITE BEST FRIEND
(AND OTHER LETTERS LEFT UNSAID)

MY WHITE BEST FRIEND

BY RACHEL DE-LAHAY

(AND OTHER LETTERS LEFT UNSAID)

OBERON BOOKS
LONDON

WWW.OBERONBOOKS.COM

This edition published in 2020 by Oberon Books
Bloomsbury Publishing Plc
50 Bedford Square, London, WC1B 3DP, UK

Originally published in 2019 as a limited edition for The Bunker Theatre

A catalogue record for this book is available from the British Library.

Cover design © David Ralf

PB ISBN: 9781786829016
E ISBN: 9781786829009

Printed and bound in Great Britain

10 9 8 7 6 5 4 3 2 1

CONTENTS

CONTENTS

A couple of years ago I was commissioned to write a short for The Bush Theatre, for their *Black Lives, Black Words* festival. I could have written a million things about Black lives with Black words and have them performed by some of the best Black talent Britain has to offer; yet there I was handing over a letter, prioritising a white actress, not doing my usual trick of hiding my truths in the voices of a million characters, but exposing them – myself – blatantly. An idea had landed that if I could put my words into someone else's mouth, I could maybe take a punt on what they might say. And if I spoke on behalf of this actor – guessed their words, their feelings – when would it stop being fun for them? And at that point would – *could* – a white person finally hear what I have to say?

Damn. Let's see if this works.

And then the show goes up. And then the DMs start. Sent from audience members, friends – friends of audience members, wanting to write their own letter. They too had things to say about privilege, parenthood, feminism, being a white man – you name it. They wanted to keep this conversation going. Only they wanted it in the DMs. Chris Sonnex, however, had started to wonder what it could look like out in the world. And so, with the support of our brilliant director Milli Bhatia, our festival was born: *Other Letters Left Unsaid*.

Thank you to all the writers for sharing your stories – for having the courage to say what is, more often than not, left unsaid.

Rachel De-lahay
November 2019

My White Best Friend (And Other Letters Left Unsaid) was originally commissioned by The Bunker Theatre and was curated by Rachel De-lahay, Milli Bhatia and Chris Sonnex.

March 2019
Artistic Director: Chris Sonnex
Director: Milli Bhatia
Designer: Khadija Raza
DJ & Sound: Duramaney Kamara
Stage Manager: Sylvia Darkwa Ohemeng
Assistant Stage Manager: Sam Hackney-Ring
Lighting & Production: Hannah Roza Fisher
Producer: David Ralf
With thanks to: Tim Kelly, Jida Akil, Georgiana Barcan, Gabrielle Lockett, Chloë Abley, Chloe Nelkin Consulting

November 2019
Artistic Director: Chris Sonnex
Director: Milli Bhatia
Designer: Khadija Raza
DJ & Sound: Duramaney Kamara
Scenic Artist: Madeleine Young
Stage Manager: Constance Oak
Assistant Stage Manager: Devon Muller
Lighting & Production: Hannah Roza Fisher
Producer: David Ralf
With thanks to: Phoebe Neal

RACHEL DE-LAHAY

NOTE: This letter is to be held and read aloud by the named actor as though her diary, written by somebody else.

First up, a request from the writer… Can we just do a quick audience reshuffle? For fairness. Just to see white, able-bodied men fall back.

Not to segregate. With our little shuffle we're just saying, we know what's going on out there, but in here, this space is safe and you are more than valued and loved. Thank you.

So… I am going to read something. Apparently.

My White Best Friend. By Rachel De-lahay.

Right. This is Rachel 'doing' me. If that makes sense? Hopefully it will. Okay…

Hi! My name is ▮▮▮▮▮▮▮▮▮▮▮. I'm best friends with Rachel De-lahay.

Best.

I'm also an actor hence... And I'm stood here representing myself. Literally. And also every other white friend of Rachel's.

Ever.

In Birmingham, where Rachel is from, her friends were mainly Black and Asian, but she doesn't see them that much nowadays. They text and FaceTime, and she goes back, though not as often as she'd like, 'cause, you know... life. So she misses them. A lot.

But it's okay 'cause we... The collective of me and Rachel's other white friends... *We* met, nearly thirteen years ago.

Wow. Thirteen years.

We've lived together, got drunk together, experimented with drugs together, fallen in love with each other, seen each other fall in love with others. Helped mend heartbreak. Fought. My God, have we fought. Laughed, cried, sang, to Britney and Rihanna, at the top of our voices, in our bedrooms, in pyjamas, on an exclusive diet of Blossom Hill.

Rachel once held back my hair as I threw up on the night bus.

I was vomiting between my legs after having one too many free glasses of Cristal in the VIP section of China Whites. I said it then, I'll say it again, Cristal is literally wasted on twenty-one-year-olds who drink Lambrini when getting ready.

We started a diet together, once, eating an excellent three-bean casserole that I prepared. Then on our way to a gig Rachel nearly passed out on the tube from 'weakness' and I had to get her off, and buy her a king-size Twix.

I borrowed her dress on holiday and it looked better on me and she hated me for it.

Then the day Rachel found out she was going to be paid to rewrite her first ever play, I was with her. In Chanel on Bond Street.

We were staring at the life we wanted and when she got off the phone we sat down in front of a quilted, navy, lambskin, two-fifty-five flap bag and thought...*one step closer.*

Then a sales assistant started talking to us and somehow got us confused with people who were legitimately capable of buying said bag so we quickly left, and went to The Botanist where I bought us a Bellini. Mine orange, Rachel's red.

What I'm saying is, I can't replace her decades-long friendships from back home. I can't be Neetu or Daina, who are both fucking ace. I've met them, lots. But we have known each other for a really long time now and we are...family.

•

The first time I met her other 'family', her 'Daina and Neetu', they came down together for the birthday party of one of the girls from our drama school. Well, they came down to see Rachel, and Rachel dictated the circumstances. So...we were gonna all hang for the first time.

I was a little nervous, as anyone is when they're about to meet the friends of your new *best* friend. You wonder if...it's gonna work, basically. If there'll be jealousy, a jostling of position. But there wasn't. Really. It was easy.

Me and Neetu got told off, quite vehemently, by Rachel, for pouring and drinking Malibu and Coke in the back of Rachel's car, after we *promised* we wouldn't, 'cause… 'We understood there was literally no way to guarantee we wouldn't spill any.' Which we did. Lots.

But Neetu laughed which allowed me to laugh, as Neetu had known Rachel for way longer so… That was the start of cementing me and Neets.

Then Daina asked me where I was from, and I said Nottingham, and for the rest of the night I became Daphne – as in *Frasier*. And… I'm not gonna lie, I'm kinda easy. Nickname me, I'm yours. So yeah…that cemented us.

I was one of the girls.

Did I notice they were brown and Black girls? Yes. Did I care? No.

So we go to the party and, no judgement, Neetu and Daina peaked and crashed hard. I was in charge of pouring in the back of the car so I take a bit of responsibility but…I was still standing, so…

Rachel had to put them both to bed and then came back down and it was back to being us, the drama school lot. And everyone rushed to tell Rachel how ace her Birmingham friends were, but equally we were kinda okay with them being in bed and there being no more outsiders.

I think I said this to Rachel, as a way of flattering her. Exaggerating a kind of jealousy. And she smiled and pretended to be flattered.

And then we danced.

The next time they were down, they'd bought tickets to some club night in Elephant that they'd had to book months in advance, with named DJs and celebrity PAs and singers or… I mean, I don't know. I'd never even heard of it. But I wasn't going anyway, 'cause I was hideously hungover and more than happy to spend the entire evening in pyjamas with zero plans.

Until Neetu and Daina arrived…

Then there was music and getting ready and Lambrini, obvs. And then…yeah, I wanted to go.

So I asked. And of course everyone screamed YES. It was Daphne!

Even though sourcing an extra ticket proved nigh on impossible, Daina knew someone, who knew someone, so…

We were off. To a typical club, that was to be playing typical music… Only the whole thing was less than typical.

There was this queue outside that seemed to snake all the way around the building. And these cars, parked up front, blaring… bass. And these loud girls…in these…tiny…. I mean, I'm all for short shorts but… I dunno.

It just wasn't…typical.

No one was really drinking… Instead there were these moody guys stood in corners, blocking pathways and toilets to just stare and smoke.

Inside! Smoking?!

Beneath their hoodies and attitudes… And the girls weren't much different.

I didn't get the big deal. Why would you plan for this?

A song that me and Rachel had said was our song suddenly boomed out and Rach grabbed my hips and pushed me onto the dance floor but everyone was dancing so…wild, and I couldn't dance like…that, so I just…

I really was tired. And hungover and I reckoned it was just my time to crash.

But Neetu grabs my arm to try and make me dance with her… And Daina is like, 'Daphne! You need another shot!' But I didn't. I needed to go. And then Rachel saw it too. So she dropped me home.

In the car we mainly drove in silence. I thanked her. A lot. And apologized for being a *hassle*. And when we got home I said goodbye, as she was going back out, and then said 'I love you', 'cause…

And though she didn't say it back, she smiled, so…

·

Most recently, when Neetu and Daina came down, we had an impromptu house party. As in, we'd gone to the pub but then wanted to keep drinking for a long time after the pub closed.

So everyone ended up back at ours.

We're in the flat drinking, smoking, some people smoking things they shouldn't be. I'd guess I knew eighty-five percent of the people there. I think Rachel knew the same. But we had enough guy mates with us to feel safe about the fact that a few randoms came back, so…

Music's playing through my iPhone, then some smart alec thought to link up the sound to the TV for more volume. So my phone is switched off, the tele's switched on and it's late and on some twenty-four-hour news thing showing some sort of protest, which completely kills the vibe.

Rachel knew it was a Black Lives Matter protest against the murder of Alton Sterling; a man who was restrained by two officers and then filmed from several different angles, by several different members of the public, all showing the officers pinning down his arms and chest and head, and still then shooting him twice, dead.

She knew 'cause that was the reason Daina and Neetu had come down that day. The three of them had gone to the march.

I wasn't invited.

Had I been, I would have loved to go. But no one told me about it so I didn't know.

Anyway, we're having this party and suddenly the news is on as opposed to Beyoncé and someone screams… 'Where's the fucking music?' Then someone else goes… 'What the fuck is this?!' And a third is like… 'Why are they allowed to say that? Black Lives Matter? Like, is that not racist? Like, why do they matter more?'

And I shrugged. 'Cause, again, I didn't know.

And Neetu and Daina looked really uncomfortable. And the silence that followed, that went on for what felt like a lifetime, was eventually filled with agreements and *yeahs*. 'It's a little aggressive, kinda exclusive…' Someone muttered how *we don't get a white history month*…which is true. Then Rachel shouted from across the room… 'Are you kidding?!' And we're back to silence.

And awkward giggles and stifled laughs. And girls on their phones, pretending to text, like there's anyone to text at one a.m. And if there is, why are you here? And in the background, on the news, name after name after name of other Black men and women who'd been killed this year alone…

I had to switch it off.

I decided everyone was too drunk and high to deal with this conversation, so I turned the tele off and the music back on.

Rachel didn't have to thank me for that. She's my best friend.

.

She then sat in the corner of the room with Neetu and Daina, chastising herself for not having the words to explain to that idiot the point of Black Lives Matter. And as I joined them, I heard Neetu say… 'Maybe not every day us educating and not every day them "not knowing". Maybe some days remembering Google is free.'

And Rachel nodded, and, wanting to support, I reminded them… 'Sometimes white people don't feel it's their place to speak about race. You know?'

And Neetu and Daina smiled.

They really are the best.

Then Neetu dragged Rachel to her feet to dance 'cause… Well, we really were all too drunk to talk about this.

I ended up in the garden that night for ages talking to one of the randoms, who was kinda funny and smart and looked a little like Macaulay Culkin in a Terry Richardson photo shoot, which was, sadly, exactly my type back then. And by the time I came back in, the party was over. Everyone had left or gone to bed.

Then Rachel walks back in, in pyjamas, to clear up the last of the rubbish, so me and 'Macaulay' help. Then, when Rachel bends over in front of him, he makes just an awkward joke about us being the last two girls, so him having pick of the bunch or something...

I don't even try and hear the ending; I've already got him his coat.

But he's now mortified, and apologises straight away, first to me and then to Rachel. Then, laughing nervously, he declares he was *obviously* kidding 'cause he liked me! And Rachel wasn't even really his type. Like he'd never even dated a Black girl before. Not that he had a problem with Black girls, it was just a fancying thing. Like, he wasn't really ever into girls with dark nipples. They just weren't his...thing.

Still holding his coat, Rachel now opened the door. He left. Then I went to bed. Then...

Remember when I said we fought?

Rachel called after me, asking if she could expect my support, ever?

I thought this was really unfair, as her two examples of me being unsupportive were when dealing with men who were just too stupid or awkward or drunk to even engage with, and they didn't deserve a response. You know?

I then looked up and Neetu and Daina were now in the doorway, in their pyjamas, Daina in a Black Lives Matter tee that Rachel looked at and then scoffed, mumbling something about *that not being the only time you weren't there.*

And I couldn't just stop so I continued with...

I would have come on the march. If you wanted my support. I would have been there, but you never asked. You never told me. I didn't even know it was happening so how could I have? I'm not psychic.

And then she scoffed again.

Then Neetu passed me to get her and Daina some water and the room was now painfully quiet, so I carried on...

And I would have spoke up to that guy. About the Black Lives Matter thing. But you already did. And it got awkward. And I'm not an academic. I don't know how to phrase things. I don't know the history to things, so I don't know what to say.

And the nipple thing? That's just blatant, ignorant racism. So what could I say to that?!

And then...

I just felt horrible. And kept thinking, why is my friend making me feel like this? And her friends were just watching and clearly thinking things. And I was like, this is stupid. I'm not the enemy. I'm not racist. I've done nothing wrong. And yet I was here being shouted at like I have. And I thought, I'd never do this to her. I'd never make anyone feel like this.

Ever.

Then Rachel said...

Sorry.

'Cause I was right. It wasn't my problem. She said…

Sorry for allowing a boy's stupid comments to get to me. I know I'm better than that. I'm tougher than that. So, sorry. Sorry for allowing myself to get drunk and become weak and vulnerable to those comments. Sorry for forgetting there's no time for that. There's only time for remembering to look after yourself, 'cause no one else will. Sorry for wondering whether if he'd called me fat you would have been more vocal, 'cause that's beside the point.

And sorry for hoping the murder of young lives, constantly, consistently, would outrage you like it did me and make you want to investigate and shout and scream and be at the centre of every protest ever. Like I had to be.

Sorry for not always getting that you and your friends sometimes want me to yourself, because you love me and love spending time with me, and when that means me being the only minority in a room, again…? Shake it off.

Sorry for daring to take you to a party where you were the minority.

Sorry for not seeing that you wouldn't like that, be comfortable with that, at all, and for not trying harder to come up with a better, safer lie in advance as to why you shouldn't join us in Elephant. Sorry for being disappointed with your not getting the 'big deal' and not being capable of saying to you, when I dropped you home, I love you. 'Cause I do. I really do. I just get angry and need to learn to monitor that better. 'Cause none of this is your problem. None of it. So sorry for assuming you'd give a fuck, when you're the embodiment of every privilege I smack up against every day. With your face that's celebrated in every corner of this earth…

You seek out 'normal' shampoo and don't think to question it whilst I sit here like... Man, that must be ace, being normal.

That's Rachel's apology.

Except it wasn't, 'cause...

That fight didn't happen. At all. I just went to bed. And Rachel let me. 'Cause this is the fight you and your white best friend will never have. 'Cause how do you say to someone you love... *You let me down.*

How do you ask your white best friend to try and visibly give a damn? Change your profile picture, share that post, march! Knowing it will make them feel uncomfortable? How could you ever put your white best friend on stage and remind them that they're part of the problem? If you love them? If you never want anyone to feel for even a moment how you feel living in this world every day?

So we don't discuss it. Which means I never got to say...

I'm sorry.

I'm sorry that when you spoke your mind, I shuffled and shifted uncomfortable with the dialogue. I'm sorry that on gutsier days I argued points defending myself first and foremost, as a woman, a white woman, struggling to see the difference. I'm sorry I never thought to educate myself privately, and fight, not even alongside you, but in front of you, 'cause maybe you're tired.

This is the most uncomfortable I've ever been on stage. And I don't like it. One bit.

But maybe that's okay. Maybe not every day enjoying our privileges and coasting through life, comfortable. Maybe some days putting ourselves out there for somebody else. Standing up, loudly, visibly, for someone less privileged, and bearing the brunt of the brazen misogyny, racism and homophobia that can incur.

I am not that white woman. Yet. These words aren't my words. They are a request, an offering, from my best friend who thinks if we have the ability to reshuffle and change a small space like this, so quickly, into a safe space, *we* have the ability to change the world.

And, having had a bit of time off up until now, asking me to do my bit.

Thank you for this experience.

Rachel De-lahay is an award-winning playwright and screenwriter. Her plays include *The Westbridge*, *Routes* (Royal Court Theatre) and *Circles* (Birmingham Rep). As a screenwriter, her credits include *Kiri* (Channel 4); *The Last Hours of Laura K* (BBC); *The Feed* (Amazon); *The Eddy* (Netflix); and the final episode of *Noughts & Crosses* (BBC), based on Malorie Blackman's young adult novel.

ZIA AHMED

NOTE: Where directions are in italics, please don't read them, do them. Everything else should be read out loud.

PIECE OF PAPER 1

a request from zia.

can all black + brown people who are working class come to the front
white + working class in the middle
everyone else back row
please be honest

please wait until the audience has moved before reading on

zainab
not gona lie
uhh
i watched the video
of *my white best friend*
and i was caught in two minds
it's a bit of a headfuck
cos i'm torn

course the piece speaks to a lot of people
but there's something about it
i can't put my finger on like
i duno
did white people respond to it
because a white person was saying it?
cos maybe intentionally or not
it centres the white person
and does that mean
they only listen to things when a white person's saying it?
you know
like
like online when bare things go viral when it's a white person
saying racism is bad
but people who actually experience it get told like calm down
or stop playing the race card
or i duno
so i'm so glad you're on stage

a brown woman
my fucking mate
i love you
you're sick
we come up to see you in stratford-upon-avon
you killed it on stage
we went back to yours
you made a banging daal
in the room 4 south asian actors/writers
you me h + s
and we jus talk for ages
about how things are changing
about how things aren't changing

about changing shit
about the joy + the pain of it
this industry it's hard
being brown being working class +
how we go on
how we've known each other for so long
sometimes it feels like
let's talk about something else
but the talking helps
i know there's bare whatsapp groups
sending the tweets the articles the good news the grievances
the support in these allegiances
in these chats

in knowing there's people who got your back
just some of the things we talked about
opened out

>   *please open the ice cream tub, and read the cards in order,*
>   *one by one*

CARD 1

dear

insert name

'Half of what I say is meaningless; but I say it so that the other
half may reach you.'

white ppl love khalil gibran
badly translated rumi quotes

'The wound is where the light enters you.'

CARD 2

this is a good white
this is a good red
this is a good brown
swirl around your mouth

CARD 3

> *please adopt the 'tory power stance'* [1]
>
> *try it a few times on different parts of the stage*
>
> *pick a part of the stage you like and hold*

CARD 4

'Did Mohindra feel that it was empowering to overturn that stereotype in the final episode?

"It did feel empowering," she says, "even just from a feminist perspective: women are constantly undermined."

She continues: "We have this idea that women who wear hijabs are oppressed and do so not at their own will and that is something that we need to think about and take stock of because that is absolutely not the case."

Mohindra is not Muslim herself, her Indian family, she says, are Punjabi-Hindus, but she adds, "My grandparents grew up before the Partition, so we have a lot of family friends who are Muslim and also I have Muslim family on my mum's side, too – both my cousins are Muslim."'[2]

CARD 5

so someone racist's jus shouted it out at them
their response is
'but i'm not even from pakistan'

this ain't a quiz
bonus question
you think they give a shit?
you want your racism to come w nuance?

CARD 6

please read in what you imagine to be sajid javid's voice

@sajidjavid
'These sick Asian paedophiles are finally facing justice. I want
to commend the bravery of the victims. For too long, they were
ignored. Not on my watch. There will be no no-go areas'
5:27 PM – Oct 19, 2018

CARD 7

'David Cameron described Javid as "the brilliant Asian man
who I asked to join the Cabinet" and said "I want to hear that
title Prime Minister followed by a British Asian name."'[3]

CARD 8

please read in new york queens accent

'Oh, great. Great. Yeah. And I try to be very vocal about that
effect. That, first off, I'm whatever, a working class then middle
class Indian kid, that rap is a black art form, and that I am
guilty of appropriation. And that it makes me feel very strange.

But at the same time this is the most appropriate medium because I don't want to be performing race or performing – I'm not a clown here to, you know, appease the white. So, it's like, if I wrote a book or if I used a different medium, I feel like the audience – inevitably my audience did end up being mostly middle and upper-class white kids, but that's also just rap right now. But I chose rap because – I admit I was appropriating a black art form but it's also a working class art form.'[4]

CARD 9

the play got made
but once i saw it on stage
i couldn't stop thinking
was the voice i heard mine
or had it turned white?

you ever thought that?

CARD 10

adopt tory power stance + speak in your sajid javid voice

'Mr Deputy Speaker, I've said earlier in this house that what I'm interested in is a compliant, not a hostile environment. But when people talk about a hostile environment, what my honourable friend reminds me of is actually some of the hard-left that has actually joined the party opposite ever since the leader of the opposition became a leader, and how their anti-semitism has been tolerated and how –'

'Order, order.'

'I was talking about members of the hard-left that have created a hostile environment in their own party, and people that welcome my appointment by calling me a coconut and an Uncle Tom. And if that's something the leader of the opposition thinks is wrong, why doesn't he get on the dispatch box right now and denounce them?

Mr Deputy Speaker, I didn't think he'd want to say anything, and we know exactly what he thinks of a hostile environment in the Labour Party against people's backgrounds.'[5]

CARD 11

adopt tory power stance + speak in your sajid javid voice

@sajidjavid
'These sick Asian paedophiles are finally facing justice. I want to commend the bravery of the victims. For too long, they were ignored. Not on my watch. There will be no no-go areas'
5:27 PM – Oct 19, 2018

CARD 12

hi
i'm the lead guitarist for the british asian experience
don't quite know our own songs yet
we play covers of covers of covers

a video will play on the screen for a bit, please watch it with the audience and wait until the sound is faded out before picking up the next card

CARD 13

please read everyone except WAITER in an indian accent. the WAITER should be read in rp

MAN #1: Alright, what are we having?

MAN #2: Jamz. First up we'll have ten –

EVERYONE: Twelve!

MAN #2: No, twelve bread rolls. And bring some of that fancy stuff...

MAN #3: Butter!

MAN #2: Butter, yeah. Okay, main course. What's everyone having?

MAN #3: What's the blandest thing on the menu?

WAITER: Scampi is particularly bland, sir.

MAN #3: I'll have that, and bring a fork and knife!

MAN #2: Listen, listen, yeah. I'm going to have the same as him.

WOMAN #1: No.

MAN #2: Except I'm also going to have... prawn cocktail.

WOMAN #2: You'll regret that in the morning!

MAN #3: Gammon steak, please.

MAN #2: Jamz. Tell you what, give him the gammon steak but leave off all your crap. None of your peach halves and your pineapple rings. Not in his condition, you know what I mean.

MAN #1: The gammon steak as well. But crap on the side.

MAN #2: Mina?

WOMAN #1: Erm, could I just have the chicken curry, please.

EVERYONE: Oh, Mina! Come on!

MAN #1: It's an English restaurant, yeah. You've got to have something English. None of that spicy shite.

WOMAN #1: But you know I don't like anything too bland.

CARD 14

an actor puts her hand up
she says i wana do roles that are not asian
i'm tired of the stereotypical roles

i wana play the white roles

the writer says
i hate it when actors do that it's so frustrating
i worked my arse off to write characters who aren't white
to get these characters on stage and instead of supporting that
you're

CARD 15

adopt tory power stance + speak in your sajid javid voice

'I've been called a coconut and worse so I know how important
it is to stamp out hate.'[6]

CARD 16

adopt tory power stance + speak in your sajid javid voice

@sajidjavid
'These sick Asian paedophiles are finally facing justice. I want
to commend the bravery of the victims. For too long, they were
ignored. Not on my watch. There will be no no-go areas'
5:27 PM – Oct 19, 2018

CARD 17

brown comedian on the bbc
walks on stage
'don't worry guys
i'm not from isis'
white audience laughs
'or am i?'
white audience laughs
'isis isis isis this is the i'm not isis dance'

white audience laughs
'please love me'
white audience laughs
good browns live at the apollo

CARD 18

you write
how when you were a kid
you tried to scrub the colour of your skin
it's fucked + it's upsetting
but i can't relate
i have never wanted to be white
just equal

CARD 19

it's okay
they're jus playing the game
+ once they're in
+ they'll start making a change
+ they'll bring us in
but what if they got so used to the game
they didn't want the rules to be changed
because they'd have to learn the new ones

CARD 20

good ones part two
they told you you were one of the good browns if you told
them they were one of the
good whites
this was the only way the good whites let the good browns on stage

who's a good brown now?
who's a good white now?
you are
no you are
no you are
no you are
cos ain't no such thing as halfway crooks

CARD 21

adopt tory power stance + speak in your sajid javid voice

'When it comes to gang-based child exploitation it is self-
evident to anyone who cares to look that if you look at all the
recent high-profile cases there is a high proportion of men that
are of Pakistani heritage.'

'There could be – and I'm not saying there are – some cultural
reasons from the community that those men came from that
could lead to this type of behaviour. For me to rule something out
just because it would be considered sensitive would be wrong.'[7]

CARD 22

so all the actors are at the screening
and all the brown actors sit together
we're excited
show gona be on bbc next week
it starts
we watch all three parts
don't get me wrong it's important

but watching it
my heart sank

and i could feel the other brown actors too
it's not like we never knew
but seeing on screen
as a whole piece
we're all playing groomers
paedos villains
it's good money and that
but
i can't keep
i mean
there will be other things
uhh
but it don't feel good
yeh money's good and that
but we all know we're playing the
i mean yeh villains are fun to play
but this ain't iago or anything
this is
and the general elections are next month
and
we're
after the screening we don't say much

CARD 23

adopt tory power stance + speak in your sajid javid voice

@sajidjavid
'If Corbyn had said "Asians" or "Blacks" instead of "Zionists"
he'd be gone by now. The fact he's still there, tells us all we need
to know about what the Labour Party has become'
9:38 AM – Aug 25, 2018

CARD 24

adopt tory power stance + speak in your sajid javid voice

@sajidjavid
'These sick Asian paedophiles are finally facing justice. I want to commend the bravery of the victims. For too long, they were ignored. Not on my watch. There will be no no-go areas'
5:27 PM – Oct 19, 2018

CARD 25

brown comedian on the bbc
first joke
tumbleweed
second joke
tumbleweed
'guys i used to be muslim
until i found out about bacon'
white audience nods in approval
'i get sad thinking about all the years of eating bacon i missed'
white audience nods in approval
'bacon bacon bacon this is the i love bacon dance'
white audience laughs
'please love me'
white audience laughs

CARD 26

adopt tory power stance

in rp interviewer voice:

'To be clear, are you saying you were bullied because you were Asian?'

in your sajid javid voice:

'Yes. Yes and uh – When I was eleven, when I just started my new comprehensive school, a very, very similar incident – and it was just unavoidable, those memories uhh – flooded back for me and uh –'

in rp interviewer voice:

'A similar incident in what, you were attacked at school?'

in your sajid javid voice:

'Yes, yes, because I was Asian I was uh – I was punched / to the ground –'

in rp interviewer voice:

'/ and language was used which I imagine was pretty unpleasant.'

in your sajid javid voice:

'Yes yes that's exactly what I'm referring to.'

in rp interviewer voice:

'So were you shocked that Britain hasn't moved on since then?'

in your sajid javid voice:

'Well that's that's what I was gonna say – part of me was that – how can this kind of thing still be going on in our country? And I really felt for that uhh – th–the young boy that was involved – the Syrian boy.'[8]

CARD 27

there's a show called *hijabi monologues*
pretty self-explanatory

muslim women wearing the hijab on stage
black women brown women
speaking monologues
about whatever they want
they can allude to it or not
it's about anything and everything
families and football and prayer and paranoia
about people real people
there's a write-up in the paper
a brown woman
south asian background
her problem with the show
all the monologues were about women who wear the hijab
there wasn't one about how it's a symbol of oppression
she don't talk about islamophobia
about these women being the first attacked
hijabs snatched off
spat on
they're seen
not heard
the show's called *hijabi monologues*
hijabi
monologues

CARD 28

'Dear Mrs Begum,
Please find enclosed papers that relate to a decision taken by the
Home Secretary to deprive your daughter, Shamima Begum, of
her British citizenship.
In light of the circumstances of your daughter, the notice of the Home
Secretary's decision has been served on file today (19th February),

and the order removing her British citizenship has subsequently
been made. Copies of each are included with this letter.'

CARD 29

hi i'm a magician
i can turn invisible and hyper-visible at the same time
pick a card any card

CARD 30

i watch this play
and the writer's british
indian
and i go in
wanting it to be good
brown writer repping
and straight in
there's a muslims eating pork joke

i get it religion is not above scrutiny
it's the only one in the play tho
nothing about hinduism catholicism
it's just a joke
religion is fair game yeh
nothing to do with class
with race
from the spanish inquisition
to muslim detainees being force-fed bacon
it's just ideas

CARD 31

you write

perform
you only get white applause
who you writing for?

CARD 32

please read in bradford accent

'Indeed, the central problem with the documentary is that throughout an entire hour focused on a racialised, largely working-class, Muslim minority; questions of race, racism or class were never explicitly mentioned or interrogated in a structural way. Instead, a narrative was spun that approached the men as if they lived lives devoid of context. They were derided as 'princelings'; who were not business-minded enough to get very far in life – as contrasted with one random Gujerati family from Uganda who Mehreen has a pint with (proof they, as compared with the Mirpuris are better assimilated, by the way)…

There was no comment on the effects of structural disadvantage and racism in the employment market, racism and being 'written off'; at school, or the de-industrialisation of Bradford which has harmed employment for multiple generations. There was no mention of austerity having removed social services and support from young people's lives. No hint that intergenerational cycles of poverty may play a role.'[9]

CARD 33

on a date
talking about favourite books
they say gandhi's autobiography is the one
for real?
i'm like gandhi's a racist

what?
yeh non-violent but racist
how?
he reckoned indians were superior to black africans
gandhi the sequel
don't see black people as equal
starring scarlett johansson as gandhi
written by lena dunham
wait she don't like indians
maybe after her film about syrians

CARD 34

photoshoot for vice
south asians reclaiming their identity
henna tattoo reads
but let's not talk about class
let's not talk about caste

CARD 35

please read in bradford accent

'Ugandan-Gujeratis largely migrated from different class backgrounds with more social capital than migrants from Kashmir who came to the UK specifically due to the colonial link and the metropole calls for unskilled industrial labourers after the Second World War...

These factors were absent from the documentary in favour of an easy narrative of victim-blaming. In fact, Mehreen's reflections throughout the show insinuated that the solution to problems facing Asian men seemed to lie in making it down to the local pub more often and just thinking as if they had more social capital.'[10]

CARD 36

read as posh white man

'Well, I've never come across any of that in the Conservative Party and we've got members in my Crawley association who are Muslim, along with many other different faiths and no faith at all.

I think complacency is a very dangerous thing and I wouldn't want to strike any note of complacency, but you know I think, a party that has a Muslim as a Home Secretary is not a party that could be accused of being Islamophobic.'[11]

CARD 37

'Sajid Javid left Deutsche Bank in 2009 to pursue a career in politics. His earnings at Deutsche Bank would have been roughly £3,000,000 a year at the time he left.'[12]

CARD 38

went
college with this writer
posh pakistani via kenya
his parents always talking bout coming here with nothing in their pockets
but not how they screwed over black people for the english
retell story as rags to riches
about meritocracy
got to where i am through hard work
if you work hard too
you can get this nice car too
after 9/11 7/7

he'd pretend to be italian or spanish
he'd be like i'm not like them
they are not my friends

he distanced himself from people like me
he wrote blogs about not wanting to write about race
and now he's on all the diversity panels
getting paid
to talk about race
the white people like him
and he likes them
they tell him he's good and he's brave
he tells them thanks for having me on the panel today

CARD 39

the brown person on the panel never mentions class
not saying you didn't work hard
but please be honest about your path
if you're able to take those unpaid internships
if you got access to the bank of mum and dad
if you can afford to work for free
if you have the luxury of spending as much time as you like
doing this
and buying tickets to see everything
no clue about second jobs
third jobs
not a competition about who's worse off
i just wanted to do my job
i'm not good at being a nanny
but it's all that i got
+ i couldn't even do that i couldn't even do that
we gota pay rent

or move back home
scrape money to get a seat
in the far back row
tiny figures
further distance
everything looks the same

CARD 40

@AGlasgowGirl
'Sajid Javid eats daal with a knife and fork'
12:13 PM – 30 Apr 2018

@AyoCaesar
'Sajid Javid 100% cooks with boil-in-the-bag rice'
5:18 PM – 21 Feb 2019

@chamelibhatia
'Sajid actually keeps ice cream in the ice cream tub'
8:59 PM – 21 Feb 2019

we got jokes + taking the piss
he got revoking citizenships
another joke we keep making more
he keeps making racist laws

they say why you hate him for?
everyday i hate him more

CARD 41

working class middle class black brown
when you climb the ladder you send it back down

PIECE OF PAPER 2

hey alice
it's me zia
you haven't seen me in like two years
you must be six
shit
time goes so quick
i felt real bad for leaving
especially with your dad being away
i wanted to stay + be there for you
of course it was a job
but you meant a lot to me
i had to quit
i got sick
it was all cos of this one night

i pick you up
from nursery
in primrose hill
we go to the park
you play with your little italian mate
matteo
i sit on the bench
chill with matteo's mum
sun sets
his mum is like matteo we gota go
he cries all the way to his car
we walk to the bus
you're annoyed at me
you wanted to stay in the park
i say it's too dark and it's nearly time for dinner
we gota get home

you just stop on the bridge
you say NO
i say we gota go
you say NO
a lady with a dog walks past
you jump
you were scared of dogs
i dunno if you still are
i say if we get home now
you can watch one episode of peppa pig
you say NO. TWO
i say no. one
you say NO. TWO
i say one or none
you say FINE. ONE
we start walking
you say you can't watch it with me
because you smell
nah not having that
i say you can't say mean things to people
it's not nice
please apologise
you say NO
i say apologise
you say NO
i say fine. no peppa pig then
and i'm telling your mum you said i smell
you say i'm telling her you said i smell
we walk to the bus stop
you refuse to walk by my side
so i walk in front
keeping an eye

you walk when i don't look
but when i turn around you stop
you say i wana take the train
i say we never take the train it takes longer we're taking the bus
you say NO
i say YES
you say FINE
we reach the bus stop
one in two mins time
thank god
you sit at the stop
i sit next to you
you cross your arms
two police officers walk towards us a man and a woman
he says excuse me sir
i say yeh?
he says we've had a report from a member of public
concerned for this girl's safety
do you know her?
i say yes i'm her nanny
concerned for her safety how?
he says
do you have proof?
i say
concerned for her safety how?
he says
one
you are clearly not related
i say i'm her fuuu i'm her nanny
two
you were not walking side by side
three

she was looking behind her
i say this from a member of public?
he says what's your name sir
i say zia ahmed
he says do you have proof you're her nanny?
i say what's proof? i got her mum's number
what's your proof you're a cop?
he says once this enquiry is done i'll be happy to give you all
my details
she turns to you alice, the other officer
she says what's your name?
you tell her
she says
how old are you?
you say four
she double-takes
i say she's four she big for her age
you were you are big for your age
you look like you could be seven eight
genes your mum your dad they're big both over six footers
he says let her talk
she says
do you know this man alice?
you don't say anything
she says
alice
it's okay we're here to protect you
you don't say anything
i say protect? i can't
he says
let her speak
i look at you

and i say
it's ok alice
you say
yes
he says
what's his name alice?
you say
zia
she says
does he know your mum?
you say yes
she says
what's your mum's name?
you say
sasha
she looks at your knees
you have mud stains
she says alice
how did you get these marks on your knees?
did this man make you do anything you didn't want to do
i say are you fucking kidding me
he says sir there is no need to get aggressive if you cooperate
i say she's four what are you trying to say?
she says sir will you please let her answer?
i say she was playing hide and seek with her friend matteo in
chilcot gardens down the road and you can ring her mum sasha
and find out for yourself she's four years old there is no need
to distress her
i am her nanny
he says if you'd pass me your phone sir
i give him my phone
i say it's ringing

shit she might not answer she's at fuckin yoga
he says am i speaking to sasha alice's mum
i'm pc jenkins i'm here with zia ahmed who is claiming to be
he stops talking
he says yep
okay
no
it's nothing to do with his skin colour
i was looking out for the child's safety
okay madam
bye
he hangs up
he says okay sir she says you're her nanny
i say i know
she says we were just doing our job
i say we know why you stopped me
he says nothing to do with your skin colour we were following
up a member of the public's concern
i hope you understand
goodnight sir
he offers his hand
alice is watching
i take it
168 in two minutes
we get home
you ring the bell excited you know your mum's home
she opens the door
we walk in
she says i'm sorry you
i say you know i wouldn't let anything happen to alice
she says of course i know that
it's ridiculous

i say she seems okay
you've gone straight to the telly + put on peppa pig

the next day
i pick you up from school
one of the kids says
alice your dad's here
you get annoyed
you say he's not my dad
you get your coat and storm off
i say i'm not her dad
the kid seems baffled
he says
why do you always pick her up?
i say i'm her nanny
you're downstairs
matteo's not staying to play
so we head back
168 two mins
you look at me
you say you're not my dad
i say i never said i was
you say
i know but william said
i say
i told william i'm your nanny he knows now
we get on the bus
you don't want to sit next to me
so i stand
you say is mama gona be home?
i say no she's at work + then she's going to yoga but she'll be
home soon
it's our stop

you say i want mama
i say she'll be home soon
you say no i want mama
i say she'll be home soon alice we gota get off now
the door opens
you say NO
you don't move
i say alice
i feel the bus looking
i say alice we gota go this is our stop
she says no you're not my dad
i can't
oh god
i feel the bus looking
thinking
worried about this little girl
this little white girl
this fucking brown man
the fucking police
the fucking public
last night weren't the first time
all the fucking time
they come up to you
+ are like
are you alright?
when i'm right by your fucking side
when we're both doing fucking fine
when we're walking when we're talking
when we're smiling laughing
they're always asking
are you alright?
ticket inspector

man at bus stop
woman in the park
are you okay?
they always see you
she's with me
i'm her nanny
you carry on playing
i keep on saying
i'm her nanny
they all look at you + say bye
now someone's gona call the police again
they're gona look at your knees again
for mud stains
mud stains
mud
cos i'm what?
fuck
i pick you up
you scream
I WANT MAMA
we get off the bus
i carry you all the way home
your mum comes back
she asks
how was today?

i leave yours
i'm going over everything
i walk down the street
i can't breathe
my chest so tight
i stop
it's gettin worse

i stand on the curb
just run
into the middle of the road
no don't
don't
i bend down
i retch
nothing comes out
dry retch
tight chest
eyes red
not for this
god
oh god
i sob
i just wana do my job
but not like this
that's when i decide to quit alice
you might not give a shhhh
i mean you're six
sorry for swearing before
it's still pretty sore sometimes
my chest my throat
i've heard good things about your new nanny
she's got you into baking
i'm sure the cakes taste amazing
but we had a good run
a year + a bit
i've written a thing
it's gona be put on a stage
this is in it
maybe one day you'll get to read it

1   Belam, Martin. 'Sajid Javid and the Return of the Tory Power Stance.' *The Guardian*, 30 Apr. 2018, www.theguardian.com/politics/2018/apr/30/sajid-javid-tory-power-stance

2   Harvey, Chris. 'Bodyguard Star Anjli Mohindra: "Nadia Isn't an Islamophobic Stereotype – Playing Her Was Empowering".' *The Telegraph*, 24 Sept. 2018, www.telegraph.co.uk/tv/0/bodyguard-staranjli-mohindra-nadia-isnt-islamophobic-stereotype/

3, 12   'Sajid Javid.' *Wikipedia*, en.wikipedia.org/wiki/Sajid_Javid

4   Muhammad, Ali Shaheed, and Frannie Kelley. 'Heems: "If Someone's Got To Do It, It Should Be Me".' *NPR*, 13 Apr. 2015, www.npr.org/sections/microphonecheck/2015/04/13/399216057/heems-if-someones-got-to-do-it-it-should-be-me

5   HC Deb 2nd May 2018, Volume 640, hansard.parliament.uk/Commons/2018-05-02/debates/2EE1AB97-59E0-4924-AE57-459FA8811E4F/Windrush

6   Javid, Sajid. 'I've Been Called a Coconut and Worse so I Know How Important It Is to Stamp out Hate Crime.' *The Telegraph*, 15 Oct. 2018, www.telegraph.co.uk/politics/2018/10/15/called-coconut-worse-know-important-stamp-hate-crime/

7   '"Wrong to Ignore' Ethnicity of Grooming Gangs – Javid."' *BBC News*, 26 Dec. 2018, www.bbc.co.uk/news/uk-46684638

8   Javid, Sajid. *Today*, BBC Radio 4, 3 Dec. 2018

9, 10   Manzoor-Khan, Suhaiymah. 'The Story of British Pakistani Men, Told by a Native Informant.' *Al Jazeera*, 16 Aug. 2018, www.aljazeera.com/indepth/opinion/story-british-pakistani-men-told-native-informant-180816085534623.html

11   Smith, Henry. *BBC Politics Live*, BBC Two, 28 Feb. 2019

Zia Ahmed is a poet and playwright from North West London. He was shortlisted for Young Poet Laureate for London 2015/16 and is a former Roundhouse Poetry Slam champion. He was Writer in Residence at Paines Plough as part of Channel 4's Playwright Scheme 2017 and part of the Bush Theatre's Emerging Writers Group 2018/19. Plays include *i wanna be yours* (Paines Plough/Tamasha).

NOTE: Where directions are in italics, please don't read them, do them. Everything else should be read out loud.

> *Please take time to look at every single person in the room to check it isn't him. Genuinely start to look into everyone's eyes. Have a realisation of calmness each time you realise that one person is not him, but be definitely nervous that he could be there. You realise this is taking too long.*

Okay, actually…

> *Clear throat.*

I just want to make the announcement. If ▬▬▬▬▬▬ from Bristol, now living in London, has a ▬▬▬ degree from ▬▬▬▬▬ University and once shaved the side of my head off whilst we were drunk…is in the room, please, kindly exit.

> *Pause.*

I know you came to be like a supportive friend or something, you're really good at that, but umm…this one. You've gotta go.

> *Pause.*

No, seriously, ▮▮▮▮, if you're in the room…just stand up and go. In fact, fuck it, if anyone in this room knows ▮▮▮▮▮▮▮▮▮▮ please just politely stand up and politely walk to the exit and politely shut the door behind you…politely.

Pause.

Ok… Phew.

Clears throat.

Dear ▮▮▮▮▮▮▮▮▮▮▮… Hi ▮▮! Hey you! … Oh you! … ▮▮▮, ▮▮▮▮. ▮▮▮▮. ▮▮▮▮▮. ▮▮▮▮▮. Fuck, sorry, I don't know why writing this I've become so fucking nervous that I've added all these names that you and I have definitely never used, and slowly putting on a voice that is similar to how you would hear the dads talk at this hypothetical Bristol Rovers football match that both of us have never ever been to but pull references from so often we'd have people thinking otherwise. It's hard to get into my natural voice for this, I'm nervous, so excuse the over-exaggerated 'casual American high school' twang that may creep in as the nerves do. Alright, ▮▮▮▮.

I know you're not here. But I feel like this is one of those cathartic moments of writing to like, process and stuff as if you are here. Like, who needs therapy when you have The Bunker Theatre commissioning you to sort out your childhood shit in front of an audience, right? Even better, I don't actually have to read this as they've hired an unlucky actor to read my grammatically incorrect ramblings so like – *swoooosh* – 'bye accountability!'

▮▮▮▮, I think you probably know this, but I love you. And I can already imagine you replying back, without even a beat, saying, 'I love you too'.

But I need you to hold off on that one, cus I think that assumes we are using the same definition of love. Like, we always say 'I love you too' to people. But sometimes that feels really fucked up cus you have no idea if you're feeling the same as that other person. Like, you're using the same word – but not necessarily the same definition. Like, you're on the same ballpark, maybe the same field, probably on the same side of the pitch – wait why the fuck am I using all these football references – but…to finish what I started…I don't know if we are aiming for the same goal.

Like, when a mother says to a toddler, 'I love you' and the toddler says, barely audible syllables, 'I love you too, Mummy'… Yes, they are on the same field, but ask the two to define the love they are feeling and we know it would be so different.

This isn't bad, just true. And I feel that for a long time, ████, we've been using the same word to possibly mean different things.

You've told me you loved me since we were fourteen, and ever since then you've said it quite a lot. I probably hear it the most from you than anyone else in my life. The first time you told me was after I came out to you on your bed after a night out. We'd lied to our parents and said we were going to the movies, but we went to a house party and drank loads of cider and then I stayed at yours because I would often stay at yours cus you lived closer to all the cool people that threw parties.

I came out and you said, 'Duh, don't worry. I love you,' or something like that.

I think the forty-third time you told me you loved me was when I came out as something else a few years later. You said something similar. 'Yeah, don't worry, I love you!!' Always with such ease.

Those examples of 'I love you' were a lot clearer. The 'I love you' felt a lot more simple. Definitive. Like, with a beginning and an end. We're best friends. We spent every day together from the age of twelve to eighteen, and still see each other now… Countless festivals. Drinking. Break-ups. Family dinners. I could walk in your house when you weren't there and just sit with your family for hours. I was there when she died. You were there when my cat died. We'd be each other's wing person to every single social event. Watched movies non-stop, just like, you know, best fucking friends. 'I love you' doesn't feel weird like that. Like, in that context, of course we both love each other.

I also want to make it really fucking clear that I don't fall in love with straight people. Not only do I find the notion of heterosexuality a natural repellent, but I also do not fully understand straight people to fall in love with them. I had too many early examples of bad blowjobs turning to shame turning to managing their disgust and hiding their insecurities, that by the age of sixteen I was already completely over doing the whole 'queer-chases-straight rom-com-turned-horror fantasy'. So if you thought you were listening to that, I know I may not be in the room right now, but please give me more fucking depth.

So, ████, it was not confusing at all when you said 'you love me too' because you were straight. So I got how this worked. I didn't allow possibilities of love to expand anywhere beyond the platonic football pitch our affection played on.

Fuck, why – whenever I enter the possibilities of bromance depiction – do these basic football metaphors refuse to leave me? Even when you think you're over it, masculinity's fragility shows up in the most weird fucking ways.

Anyway, ████, when you came out to me a year ago I wish with everything in me that I could go back and say, 'Well duh, of course, I love you,' without missing a beat, just like you did with me. I wish I could be so unphased, selfless, centring all and only you – that all I thought about in that moment was making you feel loved, better, cared for, and supported in your newest discovery.

But a missed beat. Two, in fact. You told me you were queer. Two beats went past. And then I said: 'Well, thank fuck, all the best people are. I knew I didn't have one straight friend.'

You laughed. We embraced. Cuddled a bit. And then went on to talk about all the people you may or may not want to sleep with now, exploration, re-lived-over-and-over-again awkward stories of my first queer adventures – you already knowing the endings of them word for word, but sometimes nostalgia is the best form of comfort.

I know you noticed the missed beats too. Although only seconds in length, when you are used to being in sync with one another, even the slightest slip of hand feels like a tectonic plate shifting between you. We get back on course, but when nothing's felt amiss before, we both are still remembering the gap that just appeared. I could feel us try and get our hands clicking together again. It took a few minutes.

I wonder if you thought, in those two beats, that I was a raging homophobe? I don't know, like, despite being a fucking faghot myself, that I had this 'only queer in the village' vibe attached to me, and that in those two beats I was managing the realisation of not being the only queer round your dinner table with your family?

I wonder if you thought, in those two beats, that I was... Jealous? Judgemental? Angry? I'm not sure. But I know you noticed them, and I fucking hate that I haven't been able to tell you what filled those two beats. Like, maybe tried shouting at you on the dance floor later that night, or for breakfast the next day before asking if you wanted orange juice. But sometimes it feels like if you miss your chance at the perfect shot, your kick is off-balance for the rest of the game.

Roll eyes when you notice it is another football metaphor.

If I'm honest, there was too much to say in those two beats that would ever fit on a dance floor over an over-used house beat. How can, 'and now I'm thinking of all the times you hugged me to sleep with a slightly different intention' fit within two beats?

In truth, when you said you weren't straight, I felt my mind refocus on minuscule moments we had shared together the past ten years, home in on the specifics, the touch, the look, the grab, and watch as my possibilities for love were expanded. They were only closed when they were not an option. As if love works in neat borders. As if borders are ever neat. As if they help anyone. In that beat I transported myself to when we were fifteen years old and it was another 'staying at yours after a party' night. We floated in unison from our friends' front door, back to your bed, clothes off (purely for temperature reasons), and glided into uniform positions we knew so well. You on the right side, facing me. Me on the left side, facing the door. 'I'm too drunk, let's recap the night tomorrow.' 'Sure,' I said.

I went to stretch my leg out, worried about cramps, and was met with your leg touching mine. Closer than I'd thought. I went to pull back. It wasn't the touching that was odd, more that when we were drunk our sleeping habits were often not physically close. We had a rhythm. It worked. Why change the beat?

I went to pull back my leg, maybe I muttered 'sorry', but before I even could you pulled it closer. With me. And said goodnight.

Normally, when I wake up, it doesn't matter how comfy the cuddle or embrace of the person I'm with is – I will have always broken free during the night. Call it night terrors, a fear of the other person leaving first, or just never wanting to be tied down, but waking up in the same embrace is not something I deem romantic – more just modern-day, romanticised entrapment.

That morning I woke up and you were still holding me. I did not feel trapped. You said good morning, breath smelling of no regret – just ash and beer – and carried on with last night's recap, as if the embrace was nothing for the headlines. I followed your lead. I did not miss a beat.

Fuck, you know, saying this out loud to metaphorical you, and the quite REAL room of people in the theatre, makes even me want to shout – 'For fuck's sake you adorable fags, you both love each other, just kiss!!! Get the fuck over your teen drama and just ask if you both feel the same!!'

Fuck, if I was listening to this I'd be rolling my eyes, too? Saying – is this really what is occupying your mind? But I guess it's not, most of the time, it's not at all.

But when I was told I was meant to write a letter to a best friend – something that felt unsettled – something that maybe felt like it needed to be discussed… I thought about how they'd expect me to write it to the cisgender friends, or about some deep political message, but all that came to my mind was you.

Every single time.

This feels unsettled. It feels like it needs to be discussed. It feels like if it doesn't, we will carry on with our lives and never know if the beats we are both missing form some kind of perfect harmony…or just a fucking cheesy metaphor at least. I've never, ever, written about love before. I've never found it interesting enough to write about. Something so universal yet so distinctly personal feels like inevitable failure when writing about it. But here I fucking am. Writing about you. Which, in turn, is writing about love. And I know if you were still in the room now you'd be fucking pissing yourself at this. 'Oh of course you choose a commission from a theatre to be the moment you delve into our complicated intimacy, this ain't even the main fucking show, don't you think our love story deserves more than a curtain raiser?' You always were way more casual. But if I try to imagine what else you'd say, I think it'd sound something like this:

'Travis, of course this is complicated, because people are.' And you'd touch my cheek. 'Why are you trying to box the very things that we've always been so proud of not boxing? Isn't it you who told me that humans are obsessed with binaries? With black and white. With male and female. With yes and no. With taken and single. Wasn't it always you that was so proud of existing in liminal spaces?

So why is love any different? I've already told you, since we were thirteen, that I love you. And that's never been a lie. I've not hidden it. We've cared for each other; are the first person each of us rings when something's wrong; have changed airplane flights to suit each other, cancelled parties to console each other, always been the front row at every new show you've put on (well, until you told me to leave this one), cooked for you, cuddled you, been there for you… That sounds like love to me? I'm not sure if obsessing over phrases, terminologies, what 'kind of love' this is – feels worthwhile? When have you ever been the type of person to want to define things so rigidly? You say that that's what people do when they are scared. You said 'people are scared so they box things into male and female' – well, I think right now you are scared, so you are trying to box a relationship that has always succeeded because it was doing the exact opposite. Intimacy has the power to break down walls, fuck up systems, stop street lights, halt traffic. We've proven so many people wrong just by our intimacy – why the fuck would we wanna make it understandable now? So, you ask me if I love you – I say yes, and nothing really changes. We both don't want the kind of relationship where we suddenly get a cat, and a house, and two and half annoying fucking kids. We'd still go out partying, kiss other people, meet other things, and somehow, always find our way back in unison – in bed together. Me facing you, and you facing the door.

I think that we are playing the same game, you are just using a different word to define it.

Call it football, whilst I call it soccer,

I'm not sure when you've become so obsessed with rhythms and beats,

because you've always been a bit offside to me –

and I think it was you who told me that most of life's greatest adventures are found in the uncertainty of definitions…'

Travis Alabanza is a writer, performer and theatre-maker. Their show *Burgerz* (Hackney Showroom) won the Total Theatre Award at the Edinburgh Fringe Festival as well as selling out numerous venues including Southbank Centre and Traverse Theatre. Alabanza has been listed in the *Evening Standard* as one of the twenty-five most influential Londoners under twenty-five and placed on the Dazed100 list.

Hey everyone. My name is Alison. I'm an amalgamation of every white friend that Fati has ever had. Since we're all the same, right? Lol. The bitch always wants to talk about how racist it is to lump people together, and here she is, doing it. Anyways, I've known Fati my whole life. Like, my whole ass life. Like, from when she first moved to Cambridge from New York in the first grade. Sure, I get that 'theoretically' or whatever there's a part to your life that's before the first grade so I didn't know her my real whole-ass life, but it's not like anyone remembers the years before you're in first grade anyways, so I pretty much have known her my whole-ass life. So yeah. We're twenty-nine now. In our last year of our fucking twenties. But I've known this bitch before anyone can say that they've known this bitch, so it suffices to say that we've been in this shit forever.

In the first grade she transferred in the middle of winter to our classroom, to Ms Sequerra's class. Kids didn't really do that, you know, you kind of started the year all together or you waited to be in the next grade. But there she was: middle of winter, wearing purple rain boots and a frilly pink dress, standing at the front of the class being introduced to everyone. She sat by herself and Ms Sequerra asked us all to be nice to her. When I asked why she was coming in late, Ms Sequerra told me that her parents had died, and she was living in Cambridge now because she was living with her uncle. I didn't really know then what it meant for something to be dead, but I knew that whenever I got to visit my uncles I always got to eat cake at dessert, and maybe she would have extra cake for her lunch, so I decided that I would be her friend.

She didn't have extra cake at lunch. She was part of the free lunch program so she lined up for lunch like all the other kids from North Cambridge to get their lunch handed to them on a Styrofoam board. We went to Tobin, and Tobin was between North Cambridge and West Cambridge. I lived in West Cambridge, which meant that my mom could walk to school to pick me up. The kids from North Cambridge had to take a bus since they had to go through Dannehey to get home, and no one was gonna pick them up. My mom said that not everyone who lived in North Cambridge lived in Section 8 housing, and you couldn't really go around and ask if they lived in Section 8 because that was rude, but you could tell if they lived in Section 8 because they got free lunch.

So Fati got free lunch and I decided to be her friend even though she didn't have extra cake at lunch because she was nice and mostly quiet, though she'd randomly cry a lot and when she started it would be hard to get her to stop. We'd just be in the library and then she'd be crying, and she wouldn't listen to anyone, and the teacher would have to get her older sister to come and sit with her for a while until she calmed down. But we all did weird shit back then, I guess – I would rub my boogers into the boys' I liked T-shirts, so they'd always have a part of me on them. We were fucking little weirdos, everyone who is a kid is a weirdo, and over time you just shed that weirdness. Like, for example, Fati always wore those purple rain boots and that pink frilly dress. And one day Ms Sequerra got so mad at it she told Fati that she needed to stop wearing those rain boots everyday or her feet would get fungus and that she needed to wash that dress out. And Fati cried and I was so mad because we all knew that Fati cried a lot and I didn't think it was right for Ms Sequerra to be making Fati cry when it could be avoided.

So when I got home I told my mom and we pulled a bunch of my old clothes and shoes aside and the next day at school my mom came and brought them to Fati and before class we went into the bathroom together. And we gave her the clothes and tried out a few different combinations of shirts and sweaters and pants, and put the rest of the clothes in her cubby for her to take home. And after that, Ms Sequerra couldn't say shit about shit.

And we kind of spent all of elementary school like that, inseparable. For Fati's sixth grade birthday party we all went to Walex, a roller skating park with an arcade game. Fati's uncle wasn't around a lot, but he took the night off for this and drove us all to the park. There were ten of us crammed in the car and he told us not to tell our parents, and we promised not to, and it was so fun: sitting on each other's laps, Fati and her sister sitting on the floor of the car, all of us howling on the way to the park. That was what it was always like with Fati: we could make everything out of nothing, we just all had to be a little closer together, squeeze in a little tighter, to do it.

In eighth grade we were in different classes and we stopped hanging out as much, but in high school we both went to Rindge, which was where all the kids from all the elementary schools across Cambridge converged together. It wasn't just the kids from NC and West anymore, but we had kids from East, Port, Mid, and Coast too. It was funny, the way that under the same roof we all sank into our divides even more – anytime a kid of color saw a white kid they'd assume that they grew up in West, and we had to tell them that no, not every white kid is from West. There were pockets of white kids scattered through Cambridgeport and North, and there were also the East Cambridge white kids, though everyone knew that they were on Section 8, and there was no way that anyone would confuse an East Cambridge white kid for a West Cambridge white kid since they were poor and sagged their pants and wore big white t-shirts and silver chains and got their line-ups from Dominican barbers. No one in West Cambridge got line-ups, we got haircuts. So, we were different.

But our school was on academic probation and in danger of having our degrees not count, and that made us a little unruly. There were so many of us there, from so many different places, melting pot and all that good old American shit, but sometimes it was just suffocating, being all there under that moldy roof. Like, for example passing period was impossible: all those sweaty kids crammed together trying to get to the opposite end of the school in under four minutes. And one day Ben and I were trying to make it to theater, and we were all piled in on the overpass trying to make it over to the arts building, and a group of kids started shouting 'NC' and then another group started shouting 'East Side' and someone decked someone in the face and before you knew it, there was a full on brawl on the overpass and everyone was swinging at everyone, because for some reason everyone knew where everyone was from. And it wasn't as simple as one-race-vs-the-rest: yes, everyone in West was white, but the other neighborhoods were a mess. You had the Black and Indian and Dominican kids from NC fighting the Puerto Rican and Chinese and Eritrean kids from Port – it was all a fucking shit show that made no sense to anyone who wasn't us. When me and Ben finally escaped and the hallway was completely deserted and we knew that we'd be in trouble for being late anyway, when we knew everyone else was in class so they couldn't hear us, we ambled to class screaming 'West Side' throughout the halls, something we wouldn't dare say in front of the other kids because we knew we'd be punched in the face.

We were the fully white neighborhood, and by default, the most uncool. It was funny – my family was starting to struggle financially, but my mom told me not to tell any of my West friends that. That they would look at us different. And she had to keep trying to sell off our furniture and stuff to keep the house the way it was, because she wanted to keep me in West. I mean, being in West was great. There was just more space, and we threw better parties because folks' parents were out of town, or didn't really care, and had fully stocked liquor cabinets. Our school was so big that we were divided into smaller schools inside. And all those small schools had a rep. Like, School 4 was where all the Haitian kids went because their guidance counselor spoke French and could talk to their parents. And School 5, where I was, was mostly West Cambridge kids because it was the only school that taught Latin and all of us wanted to be in it because our parents told us that colleges would like that better. And we had all the best teachers – our school consistently tested higher than all the other schools at Rindge. And also, we had our own private charted bus. Haha. Like, all the West Cambridge adults got annoyed at riding the public city busses with the high school kids because we were annoying, so they campaigned to get us our own bus that was a city bus but would come and pick up all the kids in high school and then drop us off right at the school. And we got to ride it for free. But all the other neighborhoods, the kids would have to wait for the regular city busses and pay and walk through Harvard Yard from the bus station to school. Our bus was all us West kids, but we also knew to never mention it to anyone else, you know? I don't know why, but we just knew that they'd probably make a big deal out of it, and then maybe we wouldn't have it anymore because the other kids in the city didn't have it. So being in West had all these advantages, and yeah I could see why my mom was fighting to keep me there, but here I was, wishing that we could live anywhere else so that I could scream 'NC' or 'East Side' along with any of the other groups in the hallway.

Ben and I did theater with Fati. Every winter we auditioned for the plays and we always knew who would get the leads: it was a rotating tier between me, Ben, Sarah, John and Leah. Occasionally there would be a break out of that rotation, where someone new and fresh would come along, but that was it. And yeah, we were all from West Cambridge, but it wasn't a race thing. It just would have been weird to have someone like Fati play Charlotte in *Charlotte's Web*, you know? Fati is a Fati, not a Charlotte. And anyways, we were just better. Fati worked over the summer and Leah had been in theater camp since she was in first grade, so clearly we all knew who that role would go to. And of course I'd be the lead in *Judevine*, because it was a play about a town in rural Vermont. Like Fati wouldn't be in rural Vermont, you know? It's just common sense.

But anyways, like truly ultra-nerds, we would compete in theater. It was part of the Massachusetts Drama Guild festival where we would have to time our plays: we had forty-five minutes to do a one-act play, and five minutes for tech set-up and five minutes for tech break-down. If we went over we were disqualified. And of course we took it seriously: we all lived, ate and breathed the Drama Guild Festival. But of course, our high school was never allowed to host. We didn't 'have the capacity' or whatever, but it was really because all the other schools in the competition were super white and suburban and we were known as the 'diverse' school and everyone always acted like they were 'just so glad' that we got to participate. Whatever. Fucking pieces of shit. We were good. And they were always acting like they were better than us or like we should be lucky to be there because we had a few kids of color in our ensemble. And it wasn't even that many. Like, they didn't know what it was like to walk through our halls during passing period and only see a sprinkle of white. We were the minority at our school. But at theater, we were the majority. But it didn't matter, we didn't care: we were all together, race wasn't even a thing.

Like, we rode out for each other, you know? We were the same. I knew what it felt like to be judged for the color of my skin because I knew when folks looked at me at school they automatically knew that I was from West Cambridge and they made all these assumptions about me. And then we'd go compete in Sharon or whatever bumblefuck place in suburban Mass, and all these rich white kids thought they were better than us because they were richer, and whiter. I remember walking down the halls of Newton when we were competing there with Fati and everyone just looking at us, sizing us up, all these white girls with ribbons tying their blonde hair. And their look was clear: you're not us, you can't be us.

So, we were forged through fire. And for four years we were like that: the same, all of us, showing up to these festivals and knowing that we'd be treated like second-class citizens. And our senior year we did *Medea*. And it was a huge deal because Miriana, who was Chinese, was the Medea. I don't really know how that happened, but it was also like, the most kids of color who had ever auditioned for the play. Maybe they all talked to each other about it and decided they wanted to do theater this year – I don't know. So the chorus was stacked with all these women of color, and we had to have all these extra rehearsals to make sure that we worked together in unison. And we got super fucking close. We were like this little colorblind family. And we just knew that it had to be our year – we were gonna make it to finals. We knew that we were going to. Our shit was just so good.

And we went up against St Johns, a prep school for boys, and their whole cast was…well, these white dudes. And our whole cast was like, women of color. And they were doing *The Bacchae*. And we were like, you can't be fucking serious – two schools doing fucking Greek plays, head-to-head? And you know, of course they moved on ahead. And we were pushed out of the competition. But whatever, you know? Like we were better than them. We were better.

And then we graduated, and Fati got a full-ride to college. And I was like, so fucking proud of her. You know, we graduated and Cambridge was changing so much. It was right at the start of the early tech boom, 2007, when we didn't quite know what gentrification was then, but noticed that every three months entire parts of the city looked different. And when we graduated, my family couldn't afford to live in West anymore, so we had to move to Watertown. Cambridge was getting expensive, and more and more families were being pushed out. I was the only one in West I knew to go, but I could see it happening all over the city, in other parts. Anyone who wasn't on Section 8 or upper middle class was losing their ability to live in the city. And all these young, tech folks were pouring in.

I was kind of in and out of school – it was expensive and hard to balance with my family's financial shit. And you know, Fati kind of stopped coming home. She went to Brown, and that was so amazing – for her to be at an Ivy. But she started to make all these other friends and when she would come home they'd talk about colonization and institutionalized racism, and yeah, that stuff was important, but it was like all the time, and her new friends would kind of look at me funny sometimes, and it was like – wait, I'm one of you. You know? Like, yeah I'm white, but I'm not white like those suburban kids with ribbons in their hair who treated us like shit. But cool, Fati's friends didn't really know me like that, so I understood that maybe they wouldn't see that, but then Fati started to look at me like that too. And I was like, wait what? Bitch, I know you. I've been known you. Since you first moved here with your purple rain boots. But now, you have this fancy language and you're looking at me like I'm the enemy. And I wanted to talk to her, to say that to her, but I couldn't, because that's not really what we did and when she would come home she'd come with these new friends and it was hard to get to her, you know, to get her time just one-on-one.

And so the years kind of just slipped by. And every year she was more in her life and I was more in mine, and we'd be like, 'Oh my God, you're so cute' on Instagram or whatever, but that didn't always feel real. And then, for the first time in like ever, Fati came home for Christmas and all of our old theater friends were home for Christmas and it was like, oh my God, we have to see each other. We had to.

So I threw a little cocktail party and everyone came back to my place – I was back in West Cambridge again because I was renting part of my friend's family's house, and it felt like being in high school again. And Fati came and was kind of surprised, because she was like, wait, I thought this was a theater party – where's Miriana? Where's everyone from *Medea*? And I was like – oh yeah, I mean we loved those people but they were only with us for one production, you know? Like the folks here are really the theater folks. And I mean, yeah, Fati was the only non-white person invited, but that wasn't intentional, that was just something that happened, you know?

But we start drinking, and everything is going all easy and whatever and we start talking about high school and Ben brings up the West Cambridge bus, and everyone starts laughing. And Fati looks confused, because she didn't grow up in West and isn't in on the joke, so we explain it to her, and then her face just kind of falls. And she's like – wait, what? You all had a private chartered bus to school that you didn't have to pay for? And we were like hahahaha yeah. But Fati wasn't laughing. She was just kind of staring at her glass of wine. And then she starts talking about structural racism and Ben starts arguing with her, because he's like, how can this be racist? It's just a bus. We rode it like ten years ago, Fati. And she's like, trying to say that all the other kids of color in the city had to pay for the bus, and how sometimes that was really hard, like it was like, sometimes making a decision between lunch money and bus money, and she starts talking about how there was all these other things that happened in school where the white kids from West got these perks, and we're all like woah, woah, slow down, we're all the same. And someone brings up her scholarship, like okay you paid for the bus for four years but you didn't have to pay for university, and then it gets kinds of silent and she says she's going to go home.

And I follow her outside to wait for her Uber, and it just starts spilling out, everything that I've kept a lid on since we've graduated. I'm like, you know Fati, every time I've seen you since school it's just felt so different. Like we used to be family, you know? Like you were like my sister. But then you kept coming back and you had all this fancy language and you kept wanting to talk about race and stuff, and you kept looking at me like I was fucked up, like I was racist, like something was wrong with me, but we're the same. You know? And you didn't see how hard it was for me, being white, going to a school like that. But we're the same. We had all the same opportunities and we're the same, but you kept coming back having changed because you learned something, some word that made the world make a little more sense, and expecting me to change with you, to see something that you say you saw, but I just don't always see it, you know? And I don't know why we can't go back to the way we were, when we all were just together. You know?

And she kind of looked at me, kind of sadly, and it was quiet for a little bit. And her car pulled up and I could tell she didn't want to end it like this, and I didn't want to end it like this, and she just hugged me super quick and was like, 'Yeah, Alison. I know.' And I hope she knows. I hope that wasn't just something she said.

Fatimah Asghar is a poet, filmmaker, and educator. She is the author of the full-length collection *If They Come For Us* (One World/ Random House, 2018) and the chapbook *After* (YesYes Books, 2015). She is the co-creator of *Brown Girls*, an Emmy-nominated web series that highlights friendships between women of colour, and the co-editor of *Halal If You Hear Me* (with Safia Elhillo, Haymarket, 2019).

The below is a letter popped into a suggestions box that was never responded to. Nathan is now asking me to read it, 'cause apparently, I look like the guy it was intended for. I hope that's a compliment.

To: The security guard and your pagan staff at Marks and Sparks Chiswick.

I thought I should write you a letter, dunno if you will ever hear it or read it – I mean I hope you are a theatre arty type and are in the audience tonight looking to hear some gems of wisdom… But I don't think you are, because you're a judgy, inner, basic, stupid-ass, rasclart pagan warlord!

I've been shopping at the same Marks and Sparks for two years now and you and your team of security guards *constantly* follow me around – morning, afternoon, fucking night! You would probably follow me around in my dreams if you could, but you can't because as Mr Vegas says *I am blessed!*

But hey, I'm not an unfair person. Sometimes, I get it, when I was younger I would rock in stoned as fuck, eyes all bloodshot, dry mouth, and I'm taking my sweet-ass time working out what snacks I want to yam for my reality TV marathon. FYI, I like the BBQ wings whilst I binge on *Ex on the Beach*. I move onto the giant jalapeño tortilla crisps when I watch *RuPaul's* and then mini flapjacks when I'm watching *Lindsay Lohan's Beach Club*.

Sometimes I enter the store drunk, but bouji drunk, not trashy drunk, and there is a big difference. I'll be in the shop working out what pizza will soak up all this alcohol as I'm trying to minimise how much I use Deliveroo because I don't have shares in that business when really I should.

Sometimes I enter the shop and ya boy is *hungggggoverrr* and I'm in some dirty-ass tracksuit with yesterday's top on, but let's be real, I have an afro, and I have this rule: having an afro makes you the coolest person in the room regardless of outfit. So…don't watch me.

Also what are you wearing? Your security outfit be *dead*. Some dry black suit not fitted or tailored, often has ya lunch stains on it, you lot try some basic *Men in Black* ting, with some dry black shoes that ain't even shiny. On my hangover days I usually end up buying some dirty fries and a fruit smoothie. I want health but I also need grease.

Sometimes I enter the shop sober after a long day at work and I queue up when your stupid self-service machines stop working or they want to carry on with some *Lucifer business* about 'please call for assistance'. I wait, patiently scrolling on my timeline. I'm a proper friendly customer when I speak to your lovely shop assistants, I like to ask them how their days are. The shop assistants are usually really nice.

In all of my many states I've *never* shoplifted from your store. In fact, let me let you in on a lil' secret – in my twenty-seven years I have NEVER EVER EVER shoplifted.

I know, crazy, right! The black boy with the afro has NEVER shoplifted! Let me tell you why? The main reasons are my parents!

My mum is a black Jamaican, and from when I was a child when we walked round the shops she told me to keep my hands by my side! Don't put your hands in your pockets unless your life depends on it. Don't pick things up even to look at them. Don't even scratch your damn face if you got an itch. 'But Mum how do I tell if those cookies are stale unless I give them a lil' squeeze? Or that avocado is ready unless I give it a lil' squeeze?' 'Give it a lil' squeeze with your eyes,' my mum would say. Now obvs I respect my mum but that shit makes no sense. You have to think – would a white British mum with her white kids tell them that?

I've lived by that rule my whole life sadly, which has only meant many unripe avocado and stale cookies.

Even when we wanted to pick things up and put them in the trolley, we would go get Mum and bring her to the aisle that had the Monster Munch multi-packs, then point at her to pick it up, which to be fair she always did.

My dad's white, like was-born-in-Hounslow white. He was a police officer for a while and he really has never broken a law in his life, like never ever. My dad would snitch on his own children. I'm serious, he has warned us.

My dad always said to me and my brother: if you ever wanted something enough that you would risk your *freedom* to steal it, tell me what it is and I will buy it for you as you clearly *need* it.

My dad is not a rich man. I thought that was sweet so I really never called my dad up on that because I guess I never needed anything that bad.

My brother on the other hand was like – Dad I NEED this Nintendo 64 or...... Dad I NEEEED this laptop or...... Dad I NEEEEEEEEEEED these football boots or...... As you can tell, this is prime younger brother petty antics that have paid off well for him.

I have a white northern girlfriend (her race is only relevant because of this letter). We been going out for seven years, imma get engaged this year and hopefully if she says yes get married in the next couple years. Firstly NO you and your security *rassssssssssclarts* are not invited to the wedding. I don't care even if you can get Marks and Sparks to cater for free.

Anyway going shopping with my girlfriend is different, she strolls around the shop like she belongs, she strolls around the shop like she has shares in the business, she literally picks up EVERYTHING, either to feel it, look at the ingredients, sometimes just to see the new packaging and comment on how she preferred the old packaging. The WILDEST ONE – she also will eat something when she is going round the shop, like you know when people pick up a packet of crisps and eat it round the shop and pay for it at the till at the end. When I first saw her do that my jaw hit the floor, I just thought she was trying to get my black ass tazered! She explained, it's chill babe imma pay at the end, which she always did. That's a level of Caucasian comfort that my black soul dreams of.

Here's an example of an advantage of having a white girlfriend in your store. I walked in with her the other day after a long day in the writers' room, and when I'm in store me and my lady often split, she goes one way picking shit up and I go another feeling with my eyes – also she takes proper long... Anyway I went towards the sandwiches and one of you security pagans followed me – she was white, like my girlfriend, she was quick on my heels, my hands firmly by my side, I knew I was being followed, almost expecting it. I can feel her staring, I'm not even exaggerating, my heart does speed up, it's stressful because your guards would make fucking SHIT spies, there is NOTHING subtle about it, I mean other customers can tell she is staring.

I'm looking at these sandwiches with my eyes, even though your sandwiches cost me three-fifty, even though I could technically eat one then and there and pay later and there is nothing you could do about it. I feel brave that day so I look back at her, to imply, 'I know you watching me pagan,' which makes her look at me harder. She knows what she is doing? She is following me because she believes I don't belong here, the way I look, the colour of my skin leads her to believe that I'm a criminal, I mean shit, it's that simple init... This security guard wants to be right, she wants me to shoplift right in front of her face, so that she can be right.

My lady comes up and gives me a kiss on the cheek. She found the perfect avocados. Your security guard sees this and still is staring, almost like she is like, 'Ahhhh the white girlfriend trick, I ain't going to fall for that.' I don't even know if that wallad even blinked. My lady can see that I'm being really awkward looking at sandwiches, I never take this long to pick, I usually quickly grab the Mexican chicken or hoisin duck wrap. My girlfriend turns around and sees the guard burning her soulless eyes into the back of my head.

'Imma go over to her, tell her you're a writer, tell her you got a lot of followers on Twitter, you can tweet about this.' I said, 'I BEGGGGGGG you don't do that I don't even have that many followers, imma just get my sandwich and go to the till.'

My lady cashes in on her white privilege and goes storming over to customer service, 'EXCUSE ME YOUR SECURITY GUARD IS FOLLOWING AROUND MY BLACK BOY-FRIEND, SHE IS PROFILING HIM, YOU NEED TO DO SOMETHING ABOUT THIS.' My girlfriend does that firm loud talking where the other white customers can hear. She makes a scene politely and firmly in a way only a white person could. If a black person were to do that, it would be aggressive.

The manager's face goes purple and he runs over to the security pagan and whispers in her ear. She laughs and walks off, not a big laugh, a little one to herself. The worst thing about this is that I felt that after that I had to buy the blooooodclart sandwich to prove a point.

Now you may think: why do I still keep coming to Marks and Sparks, Waitrose is better anyway. Well firstly I don't have Waitrose money yet, secondly Marks makes some nice middle-class party food and I'm here for it, but me getting followed happens in ALL shops, everywhere, so where shall I go? Shall I just forage? Well I won't because I'm black and bouji. I get the next argument – there are bigger problems in the world – Brexit, Trump, Theresa May's dance moves – BUT not feeling comfortable in life is tiring.

My best mate is a white guy (I do have black friends) who was a bit of a kleptomaniac. He is like a preppy good-looking white guy, I say this as appearance is really important to you security guards init... Like you lot love to judge a book by its cover, and don't get me wrong I do it too, I can spot a crackhead from their attire and their crack walk from miles away.

Anyway so my white mate one Crimbo was BROKE so he wrote a shopping list and went to Oxford Circus and shoplifted his whole family stuff. Now, the stuff he was shoplifting was hardly what you would expect, like he was teefing David Attenborough's autobiography, scented candles and other proper Caucasian shit! He told me on this day of robbery he had a lovvvvvvely time, as if he had bought all that shit with money. My boy is so wild he will get the shop attendant and ask them for advice before he teefs up the place. He has NEVER been caught.

I was with him one day he shoplifted from Tesco, and I was impressed and also shocked I was an accessory. I didn't even know he was gunna shoplift. If I did I would of told him, don't, I ain't trying to get my black ass tazered because you wanna teef a Kinder Bueno Easter egg.

Anyway my boy walks in the shop, he is chatting with the security guard, he picks up loads of expensive vegan shit, like almond milk, all them Quorn bits, and whatever else. One thing I did learn is that vegan shit is expensive!!!

Anyway he was talking to me the whole time, I was stoned so I bought some Doritos obvs, the cool original ones, I go to self-service, pay for my goods. I go to leave still deep in convo with him and he just walks out with this vegan hamper in his arms.

I mean even the buzzers went off, he didn't panic walk, or even buss a sweat, he just walked real calm and Caucasian out of the shop...... He did it so smooth that even I didn't realise he robbed it, he did it so calm I thought the buzzers were wrong –

it was only when he said I just teeeeefed up the gafff I told his dumb ass off...... I explained that doing that with me is brave because I'm black.

My boy explains that his style of shoplifting is 'accidental' so if anyone was to catch him he would just profusely apologise and say he's made a terrible mistake and pay for it. Now that is one of the big WINS of white privilege – you can literally label anything a mistake. 'Oh I ran him over when I was drunk but I have a PhD from Oxford...' The judge... 'Well that's out of character, that must have been a mistake.'

Let's remember black people don't make mistakes, right, that's how the world thinks.

Anyway I clicked on a link the other day that showed twenty-two celebs who shoplifted when they were famous, it was cats like Lindsey Lohan obvs and Winona Ryder, but what I noticed was that they all rich WHITE people, not one black celebrity... Which made me think, shoplifting is really not part of black culture. Not saying it's part of white culture, but I guess it's very similar to pillaging.

Now, loads of black people relate to being followed around by security guards, this is not new, and these security guards aren't always white – I've been followed around by a black security guard at your Marks shop, it's almost like you pussclarts have a picture of me in your green room. When I'm followed by a black guard that hurts the most, because they must know what it is like to be me.

I think your security guards are profiling the wrong people. Black people are PROUD, shoplifting is not something we would boast about. We are a boujiii race. We descend from kings and queens. We are EXCELLENT... Also *even* if a few of us man shoplifting from a Waitrose, Tesco, Sainsbury's etc. – just accept it's reparations and loads of these corporations pay like no tax so fuck 'em.

So, security guard mandem at Marks – rethink your approach maybe. If I had more money I would do a study and see who shoplifts the most and try to build a profile for you, because you man are WACK at it. Also you man never catch the people who actually shoplift... I see guys come in and clean all the steaks into a bag and go and shot them in the pub... More importantly, who buys a steak from a man shotting them in a pub, but that's another letter.

Lastly, I've been thinking – because of all the drama you and your pagans have put me through and because I'm petty! – I wanna shoplift one day, you have forced me to it, you have tempted me into it, you treat me like a teef so it's only right that you get teefed. I will only do it ONCE, it will probably stress me out WAY more than it will you, it won't be now as things in my career are going LIT and like I said earlier I won't be able to call it a MISTAKE, but one day, Mr Marks and Sparks, I am gunna teef a ting, and just know that you pushed me to it!

Yours Sincerely
Bouji Bryon

Wow, it really wasn't a compliment. Well, at least I can add security guard to my Spotlight.

Nathan Bryon is an award-winning writer and actor. His writing for theatre includes *Mixed Brain* (Paines Plough/tiata fahodzi, 2017) and *Dexter and Winter's Detective Agency* (Paines Plough, 2019). He has written for critically-acclaimed children's TV shows, such as *Swashbuckle*, *Apple Tree House* and *Rastamouse*, and his debut picture book *Look Up!* was published by Penguin Random House in 2019.

Sarah:

I don't hate you. How could I hate someone who is so sad? I mean, I've always thought once you hear someone's story you have to love them a little bit. At least a little bit...

Let me back up. I've had a bad boss. Like, a boss so satanic you actually start to wonder whether they were just born nasty, their glossy hair a weapon, their pointy nose your personal hell. Working for that boss honestly made me want to join the fast food industry. At least when you work at Burger King they don't text you on a Saturday asking for an at-home trauma therapist who can also do bikini waxes. I basically negotiated her divorce when I was twenty-three, because this filthy rich fifty-year-old woman was busy with a job she didn't have. She was creating a start-up that made 'joyful mirrors.' Mirrors shaped like balloons. Mirrors shaped like dogs. Mirrors that said, 'Good morning, I love you!' Basically she envisioned the most basic household item and how to give it a facelift it didn't actually need. And then she sold them for seven hundred dollars in a store her friend ran in the Hamptons. While I told her husband she never wanted to see him again. Helped her child put in a tampon for the first time. All while I was living in a hovel in Bushwick where my roommate could slide down a fire pole into my room any time she wanted just to ask if I liked her Burning Man unitard. I've been to hell. This, what I'm doing now, is not hell.

You are kind, I tell people. Almost too kind. You're constantly offering me the Celine shirt you're currently wearing or a bite of your gourmet burger or a session with your astrologer. You want me to like you. And I do, I guess. I just don't want to hang out in your bed with you all day. You 'work from bed.' You keep your laptop on a tray, put on a dressing gown, like a chubby Judy Garland with an Adderall addiction. How can you take that much Adderall and not ever get up and take a walk?

You weren't like this when I first met you. You were bubbly and productive. You woke at six a.m., did yoga, ate oatmeal. Went to the office and approved architectural plans and press releases. You had vision and charm and sassy baby blue hair.

And then, him…

Listen, I've dated some assholes. Tattooed actors. Fuckboys in girls' jeans. Guys with PhDs who never spoke, just stared into their drinks with a strained rictus of disdain. But he took the fucking cake, this dude you found. This clueless jobless cypher, a black hole of a man. Drinking your orange juice and lying on your couch, bringing his friends over to smoke weed in the office he turned into a grimy den. He must've had a cock made of birthday cake cuz I don't know… But you were sprung. You were smiling. You were over the moon and wearing lingerie to breakfast. You were all in.

You bought the engagement ring yourself. At Tiffany's on a Thursday morning, standing alone in a little black dress with your spanx showing while I watched you from a bench in the store. 'Do you have one with two emeralds?' you asked. 'That's our birth stone. We were born three days apart. I'm older. Cougar.'

It came to sixteen thousand dollars. 'A starter ring,' you chirped as you prepared to hand him the box so he could surprise you later. You proposed, it seems, to yourself.

The next week you caught him in bed with his French friend from his last rehab. Her name was Nuju. NUJU!!! I didn't see her but her hair was apparently down to her ass and soaking wet, like she'd just taken a quick pre-sex romp in your rain shower. It's a good fucking shower, good for you Nuju! Good for fucking you.

And he was gone. Into the night. No fight, but he took the ring. So…you sent me out for a new one. Only this one had two black diamonds. Of different shapes. His soul and your heart, you said. The same but different. 20k this time. And you asked me to sit in your bed as you tried it on.

I lay across the bed with you. You showed me your favorite YouTube videos: of cats hugging their owners, kids who can name all the presidents, a little girl reciting Maya Angelou poetry. You tried to cheer up.

Then you laid your arm across my thigh, flexed your wrist, wiggled your ring finger where the diamonds glinted in their evil way.

'It's pretty,' I told you. 'It looks…strong.'

You smiled faintly and sent me back out for your medicine.

Lena Dunham is an American filmmaker and actress. She is the creator and star of the critically-acclaimed series *Girls* (HBO). In 2013, Dunham was named one of *Time*'s most influential people in the world.

Dear ████,

I have always been a nerd, always a geek, a dweeb, one prone to attract wedgies and spit wads, a wimpy kid who was laughed AT rather than WITH, and all through childhood, my lack of cool plagued me. The bullies would smell my blood like sharks in water and swarm in. I learnt to talk fast and run even faster, from their pinches, punches, taunts and tongues.

We left Nigeria for England in 1996. I started schooling in Holland Park in London and could not shake off my dweebyness. In those early days, I tried to get my classmates to call me Phaze, instead of Inua. I don't know if it was the gold-rimmed glasses, the brick-thick African accent, the tight jeans or lack of basic hand/eye coordination, but I failed. Phaze was someone who could dribble past several defenders and score, who never tripped over his shoelaces, who had several pairs of Reebok Classics and velour tracksuits. I was too poor to be Phaze, and could not kick a ball straight. Phaze was too cool to be me. Inua stuck.

Like I said, I was good at running.

Older boys of the school would seek me out and challenge me, sometimes during lessons; they dragged me to the playgrounds to race. Perhaps all the years escaping bullies in Nigeria had paid off, my speed increased. I could move swiftly, and did so, between the various factions in school. I knew the nerds, the athletes, the artists, the basketball players and the few goths who roamed the halls like sad panthers. I hung out with them all long enough to make decent conversation, but not long enough to belong; besides, they didn't want me.

I never had a girlfriend.

I was too much of a dweeb. The only girl I liked, who I regularly spoke to, liked a boy in the year above, who always wanted to race me. She asked me to tell him about her, to put in a good word. I did. I wanted her to be happy. Even then, at fourteen, I think I understood what it meant to care for someone selflessly. She was an Iranian girl with large eyes the colour of oak, deep forests of the stuff, in which I'd try to lose myself. She'd catch me staring at her and I'd apologise. In the last week of school in Year Nine, I plucked up the courage to tell her how I truly felt.

Two weeks later, after three years, we moved to Dublin.

I was the only black boy in the entire school when I started. Ireland was in its infancy in race relations and the prejudice and ignorance I faced was treacherous. There were no places to hide or in which to attempt to fit in. I stuck out of every possible group and my dweebyness threatened to drown me. The kids who came up to me thought that being black I'd have an encyclopaedic knowledge of hip hop, or being African I had lived in mud huts or trees. I hated hip hop and was painfully middle class. I failed them desperately and they walked away disappointed.

I sought sanctuary in the art department and in my English lessons. My Irish teachers embraced the dweeb. In hindsight, because I confounded their expectations of black Africanhood, I think they saw me as a live anthropological study. They gave me the keys to the art class and entertained my ideas on literature. Slowly I learnt to own my inner dweeb, to take pride in it, to turn it into a shield and eventually into a sledge hammer.

I used that shit to run the first ever arts festival in my school. I became the Vice President of the student council and by my final year, I was appreciated, perhaps even liked by the entire student body. But there was no romance. I found out later that the one girl I had kissed in the school disco had been dared to kiss me. The week of my final year, a girl I'd known in the year above, who had left the school and so could not be influenced by its social pressures, finally plucked up the courage to tell me how she truly felt about me.

Two weeks later, after three years, we moved back to London.

We arrived in 2002. I was eighteen years old and I was lost. I had words in my head, a sense of how they could fit together, and began to write poetry. This is how we met ███████, years later.

I used to run an event called Poejazzi. Poetry and Jazz, terrible name, I know. You came with a friend. You liked what you heard of the poem I had read and remembered me. I didn't remember you, I could not have. You were beautiful. Brown eyes, long brown hair. I had learnt to ignore anyone I found attractive because life had taught me they'd always be beyond reach. My brain would filter them out automatically. The dweeb had his shield up.

We met during a workshop at a theatre in South London in February 2008. You told me where you had seen me months before and asked for my number. I was stunned. I gave it to you and we met a week later. I remember asking you: 'If you could be any week in history, which would you be, and why?' You told me that was when you knew I was a keeper.

Our first date was on Valentine's Day.

It was spectacularly perfect. Music and dancing. I learnt your fearlessness, your confidence, that you were the popular girl in school and university who could pull anyone; who did pull everyone, even your basketball coach. You were the prom queen to my nerd. You told me you had studied forum theatre. I told you I was working on a play. You told me you had schooled with Craig David in Southampton. I told you about bullies in Dublin. You asked why I had left Nigeria and I told you the whole story.

That my father was a Muslim when he married my mother, a Christian.

That my father travelled to Mecca for the pilgrimage.

That he saw something that didn't sit right with him.

That he questioned his religion when he returned.

That the local Muslims fundamentalists were not happy with this.

That they tried to hurt our family.

That we had been denied the right to live in England twice before.

That we had an immigration high court appeal coming up.

I said all this as calmly as I could, staring into your face, the dweeb in me shivering. I had never told anyone before. I was deeply embarrassed. I was terrified of what they might say or do, and the months after proved that I had been right to.

You tried to play it cool.

I explained that hundreds of thousands of people were in this situation, that my family and I would be fine. We carried on seeing each other, going out with friends, to events, typically couply things to do, but something in you had tightened and sharpened, as if you saw something pathetic in me and was quietly pulling away.

You began asking strange questions, once claimed that one in four Africans has AIDS and if I had checked myself before we slept together. There was such accusation in your eyes.

You compared me to my contemporaries, asking why I hadn't achieved what they had.

On the first scratch night of my first ever play, you went on holiday.

The further you pulled away, the more I clung to you, trying to reassure you as best as I could that everything would be okay.

I followed you to family gatherings, to the fancy dress party where your brother arrived dressed as a Nazi.

I travelled with you to Winchester, and in the car, plucked up the courage to tell you how I truly felt. That I loved you. I'll never forget your response.

You turned sharply and said, 'Don't you fucking cry.' I could have died in the chair. It seared across my chest. It stung me. You turned colder after that.

You'd go out on your own, get high on coke and refuse to tell me where you had been.

You started flirting with other men.

In February the next year, you followed me to the immigration appeal hearing and held my hand as the judges dissected the lives of my family and I, weighing our worth. I loved you harder than I ever had before for sitting through that with me, but later that night, you told me that if the result for our appeal was negative, we would break up.

A few days later the results came.

It was Valentine's Day.

Our appeal had been denied.

And just like that, we broke up.

In the moment in which I most needed to belong, you had gone.

You called the next day asking if I understood your decision. I said I did because I didn't want you to carry the weight of me, to feel guilty. But I didn't. I believed that if two people cared enough for each other, nothing could tear them apart. The break-up cut deeper than anything I had ever felt and shattered every part of me.

I swore there and then never to be around anyone who had lacked faith, who didn't believe in the impossible, and I tried to forget you.

The following year, my play transferred to the National Theatre. You were cycling across Waterloo Bridge and texted to say you'd seen my name in lights emblazoned across the city.

I did not respond.

You sent messages about five-star reviews.

I did not respond.

You would send me random texts about friends of mine you had seen.

I never responded.

The following year, my family and I battled the Home Office again and won. We were given Discretionary Leave to Remain, three years to live and work, after which our case would be reviewed.

The judges cited my work as a main factor in the outcome and I decided to make sure that after three years, they would have no choice but to allow us to stay. I worked tirelessly to root myself in this country, to convince the government we belonged. I wrote books of poems and plays. I performed, I travelled, I read, I taught, and through it all, I was haunted by you, by fears of being abandoned, of never being enough, of never belonging.

It burned like a storm of fire in me.

I'd hear your rough questions, comparing me to others. I'd imagine you in my audiences with your back turned. You were nowhere and everywhere. For years it fuelled me to be creative, to be relentless, to be black and excellent. It became unhealthy.

Last year after Valentine's Day, almost a decade to the day of our first date, you texted.

'Hey Inua.

How are you doing, lovely? It's been such a long time! I think of you from time to time and (increasingly!) your name pops up on my Facebook feed, linked to fantastically exciting achievements and wonderfully good news surrounding your poems, plays, books etc etc!!!

I've reached out to you a couple of times but you haven't responded. If you don't want to connect, that's okay. I just really want you to know (and I know that this must seem ridiculously out of the blue) that I am sorry for the way I mistreated you at times. You were such a kind and sweet lover, as gentle a boyfriend as any girl could have wished for. And I was like a lion with a thorn in her paw; always raging, always roaring and swiping.

I ask you to forgive me and I hope, one day, we can be friends again.

In the meantime I also wish you many, many more successes and that you're happy, in love and loved wholeheartedly in return.

You SO deserve every bit of kindness and praise there is.

Be well, my old friend.

 x'

The following month, twenty-four years after we ran from Nigeria, we were finally granted Indefinite Leave to Remain by the Home Office. I threw a Passport Party in Brixton, and later at night thought about you.

I wondered if perhaps, back then, you had just been scared about loving someone the world might take away from you, and you were looking for a reason to escape me.

I texted back.

'Hey ████,

I hope you are well. Thanks for the message you sent and I am sorry for taking so long to respond to it, to you, and to the ways you have reached out to me in the past.

How we ended ripped me apart, in ways you can't imagine. It haunted me and still does to some extent. It also gave me a fierce determination through various battles over the years. Some of them are still raging. Some have burnt out. Some are burning me out.

If you are still seeking forgiveness from me, you have it, and further than that, you have my understanding.

I hope you and your family are well.

Best, Inua.'

I meant every word of that message, but you should know that most of my friends now are immigrants or children of immigrants, and England has become hostile to us.

The racists, fascists and nazis smell our blood and come for us like sharks in water.

Whenever we feel like we don't belong, we know we belong to each other.

They have undone what you did.

They have shown that it is possible to be landless and loved.

That it is logical to believe in the impossible.

I do hope you are well.

Thanks for the life lesson.

Inua

Inua Ellams is a poet, playwright, performer, graphic artist and designer. He is an ambassador for the Ministry of Stories and a Fellow of the Royal Society of Literature. His poetry is published by Flipped Eye, Akashic and Nine Arches. His first play *The 14th Tale* was awarded a Fringe First at the Edinburgh International Theatre Festival and his fourth show *Barber Shop Chronicles* sold out its run at the National Theatre. His play in verse *The Half God of Rainfall* was published by Fourth Estate in 2019, and his first full collection of poems, *The Actual*, by Penned In The Margins in 2020.

NOTE: The following are real headlines, blogs, and extracts when you Google 'Forest Gate, Newham'.

Let's all move to Forest Gate
Look at it on the map and think, well, not much. But then it turns out that Forest Gate is quite Hollywood.

Fo-Gate is the new Dalston
Still think you're cool for living in Dalston? Forget it. There are hushed murmurings over M&S kombuchas that Forest Gate – or indeed Fo'Gate – has taken the crown of East London places to be if you're ahead of the curve.

Can't afford Hackney? Head for Forest Gate
Forest Gate is changing as middle-class families move in, attracted by relatively cheap houses and the imminent opening of the Crossrail station.

What makes Forest Gate so great
Residential reverie – it's close to the Olympic Village. It also has a nice community feel, with Victorian homes – and it's just twenty minutes into the City.

Buying in London? Try Forest Gate

The new London hotspot is chic, commutable and affordable – for now. Forest Gate in Newham isn't the bargain it used to be, of course, but it's better value than many London areas. With house prices at an average of £443,877, Forest Gate is cheaper than Stratford Village's £500,194.

My First Home: ███████████

'About four years ago, we [█████ and husband ████████████] bought a little terrace in Forest Gate. I'd lived in Hackney for all of my time in London and was thinking about where I could get a garden and space and as much for my money as possible while having good transport links. We wanted to future-proof the purchase… After this I'd love to buy a holiday home in France.'

Community venues breathe life into the UK's left-behind areas

The Wanstead Tap opened in early 2014 as a beer shop and café under Forest Gate railway arches. It has morphed into one of the many cultural and social hubs that have sprung up in changing communities.

Owner, Dan Clapton says, 'Prospective new residents come in almost weekly and tell us the Tap is a factor in them coming to Forest Gate.'

Clapton rejects the term gentrification. 'We've brought life here,' he says. 'When we opened there were drug dealers on the corner making local residents unhappy. Within a week they were gone because they were too exposed.'

Clapton pays his mortgage by keeping his job as the producer for *Come Dine With Me*.

Why everyone should discover The Wanstead Tap

I stumbled in just before closing, and The Wanstead Tap quenched my thirst – and saved my sanity with a can of Fourpure IPA. I still have that on a shelf in the kitchen.

*

Hey,

I know you're wondering why I wanted you to hear those headlines and extracts. You're new to the area, and I remember when your friend asked where you'd moved to, you said Forest Gate, and they said, 'Oh, I hear that's a cool place.' And you nodded, saying, 'Yeah, I love it there. It's really cool.' You said all the same things those blogs and newspapers say. You said you hadn't even heard of it before you started looking for houses. And who can blame you? It was the same for me, a few years back, when people would ask where I lived. They had only just started hearing about Newham because of the Olympics, so of course they didn't have a clue where Forest Gate was. All I could say is, 'It's close to West Ham Football Ground.' Obviously, that's not the case anymore either. But back then, they knew West Ham for the hooliganism. It's some sort of reference, I guess, isn't it?

I actually agree with the articles and with your friend. The pop-up shops are pretty nice. The railway arches look better with breweries, coffee shops and supper clubs, than they did with run-down mechanics and cheap fabric shops. They've repaved the roads, added shiny signs everywhere, and did you see how much they renovated the station? It definitely looks like a 'hot place to live'. It really is 'cool'. It's no longer a complete 'shithole'. So many people used to say that to me.

But, look, here's the thing I wanted to bring up with you. Something that's going to seem so small and insignificant. Something I'm embarrassed to even bring up with you. But, if you could hear me out, just for a few minutes. I'll make sense of it. Somehow.

It's just that I feel uncomfortable whenever you use the word 'cool' to describe the area. I don't know why but there's something about that word that cuts me deep down inside somewhere. It kind of breaks my heart. And before I tell you exactly why, can you listen to some more headlines and articles that also come up when you Google 'Forest Gate, Newham'? Just for a minute? Bear with me. Because these are real too...

*

Gentrification fears loom over rise in East London 'property millionaires'
Up until a few years ago, even the most enthusiastic estate agent might have struggled to describe some of these areas as 'highly sought-after residential locations'. However, the ripple-out effect of surging prices in other already-expensive parts of London, plus factors such as 'the Olympic effect', have pushed property values to record highs in many once-unloved boroughs.
However, with much of London now out of the reach of many buyers, some campaigners are talking about a gentrification crisis. There are concerns about the widening gap between rich and poor in some 'newly affluent' parts of London.

Newham has highest rate of fuel poverty in England, government figures reveal
Government figures reveal that 20,060 households in Newham cannot afford to heat and light their homes properly without being pushed into poverty. Rising energy costs, low incomes and energy-inefficient housing are the main factors behind

fuel poverty, according to NEA chief executive Adam Scorer. We hear about children spending most of their time at home during the winter in bed trying to keep warm, rather than socialising with their families.

Newham has the highest number of residents earning less than the London Living Wage

Director of policy at Trust for London, Manny Hothi, said: 'We all believe that work should be a route out of poverty. But almost a third of working Newham residents earn less than the real living wage.'

'Mummy, are we poor?': the destitute children denied help by councils

In the space of just a few years, increases by ████'s landlord left her paying 80% of her wages on her Forest Gate accommodation, on a monthly rent bill that jumped from £700 to £1,300.

One in four children across London has fewer than ten books of their own at home

Ten schools throughout east London, including in Newham, have been sent 6,400 books as part of an initiative to redistribute new and 'gently used' reading material. Lack of time, negative experiences as a child or lack of parental confidence about their own reading skills can all undermine a family's propensity to own books.

Newham youth worker 'felt like a criminal'

Youth worker, ████, who works in Forest Gate, has said: 'I've been searched fifteen to twenty times in five years by local police. I feel like a criminal each time.'

East Ham foodbank struggling to keep up with rising demand
A Newham charity which has delivered more than 5,500 emergency food parcels says a third of its recipients are children.

Two treated for knife wounds after Forest Gate stabbing
One of the men had a cut on his neck. His injury is not life-threatening.

Bet that's not your experience of Forest Gate, is it?

See, there's still a bunch of us who live in the area, a few streets away, and honestly, there's nothing 'cool' about this side. Because it may have the same postcode as yours, but it's a different world to the one you know. And the memories we have of the side you live on, the side that is 'cool' now, aren't different to this either.

Before it was considered 'cool', it was dirty streets, and roads with potholes. It was council estates and cold, grey concrete, not tall, shiny apartments. It was two-hour waits in GP surgeries, not getting appointments for three weeks, and attending schools because they were close by, not because they were good. It was betting shops, not breweries, and piecework factories, not fancy coffee shops. No one ever said 'cool' when they heard that you lived in Forest Gate. They said, 'Where?'

I know you must object to the term 'gentrifier'. I know you're just an individual, and I know it's the property developers that are the issue, and you're just here because you wanted a home. That's fair. After all, we all want a home, don't we?

But see, if no one cared that these streets were dirty before you got here, or noticed the potholes, and neither did they care about the overcrowded houses, and crumbling tower blocks, what is it that made them make the space for you? To clean up, and to make it 'cool'?

Is it that you can afford holiday homes in France? Is it that you have TV jobs? Is it that you can dedicate a shelf to Fourpure IPA? Is it because you're rich and white?

I know you're not colonisers. But, you know. Aren't you? Because it seems Forest Gate wasn't 'cool' until you could buy golden milk instead of haldi doodh.

See, what you see as 'cool' feels a little different to us. We're reminded of something whenever we see a new apartment block here, or a shiny new sign, or a bed of flowers being potted. Whenever we see potholes finally being filled in, cleaner roads, or a new coffee shop that has opened up. Whenever we hear the word 'cool', we remember all the things we know about the area...

We know that just like Hackney, like Brixton, like Brick Lane, Forest Gate will become so desirable, that it will become unaffordable to the communities that live there.

We know Newham is now synonymous with the 2012 Olympics and Westfield, but is still one of the most deprived boroughs in the country.

We know that the railway arches where there are now breweries and coffee shops used to house piecework factories that were run like sweatshops only a couple of decades ago, where immigrant women worked for pennies.

We know that in the name of progress and redevelopment, the 2012 Olympics forced the closure of endless local businesses in Newham without adequate compensation.

We know that the story we're sold of class is about the white working class, where immigrants and people of colour can be portrayed as the bad guy, so Brexit grievances are now legitimate but ours are not.

We know that where the new M&S has opened used to be a small grocery shop, like so many others that have disappeared.

We know that when you Google East London, Shoreditch comes up as the top choice, not where we live.

We know that the place you call 'cool' now, people just like yourselves used to make us feel embarrassed of living in.

We know that the turmeric you now love used to leave yellow stains beneath our fingernails we'd try to hide from those like you.

We know that beautiful Victorian house you've bought used to house thirty immigrant men in the seventies, who took turns to sleep after working hours in factories.

We know that despite this, a BBC documentary about the last white people in Newham can make you feel guilty, as if you're not supposed to be here.

We know there is no guilt to gentrification, because immigration is bad but gentrification is the urban version of the white man's burden, so it's okay.

We know that those who died in Grenfell Tower didn't die because they lacked common sense (fuck you Jacob Rees

Mogg), they died because they weren't worth making changes for either.

We know that the new apartments and improvement in schools, hospitals and doctor's surgeries aren't happening for us.

We know that the face of home is changing, but we know it's not for us.

We know that a place is 'cool' so long as you don't see us.

We know the pain that comes with knowing the reality of your worth to your country.

Rabiah Hussain is a playwright and screenwriter. She is a graduate of BBC Drama Room. Her critically-acclaimed debut play *Spun* ran at Arcola Theatre in 2018, receiving four-star reviews in *The Guardian* and *The Stage*, and was nominated for Best Stage Production at the Asian Media Awards. *Spun* toured Canada in 2019, and won the German Baden-Wuttemberg Youth Theatre Prize in 2020. She was a writer for the prestigious Kudos TV and Royal Court Theatre Fellowship Programme 2019.

NOTE: Where directions are in italics, please don't read them, do them. Everything else should be read out loud.

I must begin this letter by declaring that these are not the views of The Bunker Theatre or Rachel or Milli's or anyone involved in this production. The thoughts and feelings here are all alone. And I'm not here to bash anyone, I'm simply trying to reach out to a person I care about who I'm not sure... Anyway –

> *Look to tech person and nod.*
>
> *Cardi B's 'Money' plays – only the first stanza.*
>
> *Lip-sync only last line.*
>
> *Enjoy the beat, rhythm or not.*
>
> *Music abruptly stops.*

I think I'm in love with a Tory...

I don't mean Cardi – not that she's a...

I'm pretty sure I love a Tory.

Though she wasn't always one. We went to the same school, to the same college. We were in the same class but born in different years. We lived in the same borough. We were – are the same yet so different

That's what I loved – love about us.

I was her Bey and she was my Gaga.

(Funny realising how they never finished their music video trilogy, there was 'Videophone', 'Telephone' –

Anyone remember that?

I wonder what the last one would have been called? 'Voicemail' maybe?)

I remember when you finally told me you voted Conservative in the 2010 elections and I just dismissed it. I didn't understand politics then and can't say I better understand it now. We never studied it in our strict catholic school, everything was down to God and his son named Will, which we later learnt was in fact Jesus.

When May 2010 came around, in the end, I just listened to my mum who told me to vote red because she's usually right about everything else in my life – and when you have a mum like mine you do as you're told first and ask questions later.

You tried to explain your reasons and little did I know then how those reasons would soon apply to me. I was the exception to the rule until I rolled over it.

When I first started secondary school, I found it difficult to make friends but you know that. We spent the first two years eyeing each other up. That's why we didn't become friends till year nine, when you offered to wait with me till everyone had climbed the stairs to class before I ascended. You took my PE bag hoping it'd make me climb quicker,

It didn't, but you weren't fussed because you then held my bag every day till we finished college.

Our little duo grew into a trio. We were like the original Sugababes except we had a Turkish one, an English one and a Nigerian one.

You'd both say – I was the secretive one – too serious – too guarded – had walls taller than any building in London.

But *you* both climbed it and with each floor – you taught me to laugh loudly, smile broader than my face, to take the piss out of myself and my accent – yes I don't sound like someone who grew up in *the ends* but you can thank my mum for that.

> *You can say this in a Nigerian accent or one of your parents' accents:*

'This is the Queen's country and so we speak the Queen's English. Until I hear Elizabeth say "innit", I don't want to hear "innit" in my house.'

But most importantly you taught me to take the piss out of life...and boys. And so when you reached the summit, behind my steel walls, you dropped me a ladder

but when you realised how long it'd take me to climb a ladder, you switched gears and built me a lift and told me the world wasn't so scary.

I felt so lucky. Where else would you get a friendship like ours? I thought you both were magic because you turned an invisible geek into an invincible one.

You both taught me a lot about sex – like a lot – like who knew there was so much to know about sex. Like how sex doesn't just happen between your thighs, you can use fingers, tongues, heads-shoulders-knees-and-toes.

We had bonded over our single parent households and joked if we could orchestrate a *Parent Trap*-type romance between your English dad and my Nigeria mum, so we can make our sisters title legally official.

Turns out we didn't need to. My mum adopted you as soon as she saw your smile, your love for me and how well this English girl handled her spiciest fried rice and even dared to asked for more. You were Mum's fifth child.

And when you finally invited me to your yard, which sadly you couldn't build a lift in. You cheered me on every twenty-eight steps I climbed.

We joked we'd be married if we were lesbians. I'd plan our awesome *Sailor Moon*-themed wedding and eighty-day honeymoon around the world and you'd interior design our house in the country that was far away from the buzz of city life but close enough you could get into town and we'd live in blissful yet stylish matrimony.

We shared things that we will take to each other's grave, our love was otherwordly.

But then in 2017 when Tresseme announced a snap election and we were marched back to the polling stations.

I get it was hard –

Choosing the lesser of two evils.

We shouldn't have to choose evils, when we'd barely seen the good.

I'd reminisce about the days of borrowing each other tuck money or sharing lunch and trying to cheer each other up with our early Saturday morning trips to the cinema in Stratford. We'd get my mum to drop us off at nine-thirty before the cinema even opened so we could see the very first screening and have the whole screen to ourselves – we found small ways to feel big.

So months after the election I was gobsmacked when you'd told me you voted Conservative again.

And though this time round I may have been wiser

I was not louder, because this time your reasons stunned me into silence. Because if you thought that of *other* benefit claimants and those reliant on the NHS then I must've not been the exception to the rule anymore because now I was both.

You can't separate me from my condition. Disability is a part of my identity. So what makes you think you can separate your vote from your beliefs.

Did you really not know your vote would be condemning disabled people, working class, single parent families, low-income families, immigrants and benefits claimants?

I tick all those boxes.

A bounty had been put on my life and you can't pretend you didn't see the posters, the hostility, the adverts. They were – are – everywhere.

And frustratingly to this day I've not been able to broach that conversation with you. I *love* how we can agree to disagree unless our disagreements lead to arguments.

We don't speak like we used to. Daily WhatsApp messages turned to weekly WhatsApp messages turned to monthly, turned to...

Public holidays and birthday messages.

We dropped our traditions, and like a couple in troubled waters we even went on holiday together trying to save our relationship.

We both spent over a year saving, and *yes* we had an epic adventure together, but a good week can't save a bad year. Plus who wants to address difficult things on holiday, sipping non-alcoholic mimosas while lounging beside a rooftop swimming pool in thirty degree weather?

I have broken bones because of this government.

Because I wasn't given an adequate care package, because there's supposedly not enough money. The solution? Been threatened twice with being put in a care home or that my ageing mother should care for me.

In the five years I've needed a care package, they have forced me to justify my existence to the point *I've* started to question it.

Or how the NHS has saved my life and yet have also almost been the ones to take it more times than I can count.

I have been punished and financially penalised for daring to have ambitions.

I'm sorry but;

'I see it, I want it, I stunt, yellow bone it
I dream it, I work hard, I grind 'til I own it'

For daring to dream bigger than myself. I'm not sorry for that.

This government has emboldened division and tried to make me blame my background, my skin colour, my ability, even my own community, for the difficulties I've faced.

They've sold off our chances of owning property or living in a community with the people I grew up with. People like *you*.

And they've killed some of us, the ones you classed as a drain on welfare services, on the NHS, those without support and family like mine. Their voices can't be heard anymore.

We vote for those we believe in right?

I know you didn't create the dehumanising policies or enforce them. You didn't physically do any of the ills that they've done. But when you vote for a party that believes lives like mine are worthless, of no value and should not be treated as equal. Or people of my tinge should be deported even if we were born here, or granted leave to remain or given our lives to this country. You can't tell me I'm different when under the eye of this government, under the eye of society, under the eye lids of London, I'm not different. We're too old to be this naive.

I'd being lying if I said I don't care you voted Conservative, because I do. I care that your thinking became less colourful, you took back your hand, your actions became smaller, your voice quieter than still water.

When the world was raining down on me, *where were you?*

When I lost my dad, when I lost my grandma, when I was lost?

The crushing thing they don't warn you about, in friendships, is that they can be cancerous. Some people you're able to cut out, leaving only a small scar, to remind you of the now inconvenient memories your mind houses. Whilst others are a bit more complicated. You can't cut it all out at once, otherwise the consequences could be fatal. Some of it must remain inside you, because they are not just your friend anymore, they've metastasized. They're friends with your friends, friends with your family, they've become family but crucially they've made it to your heart. Not many do make it that far, which is why it can be so hard to cut them out because you will essentially end up losing a piece of yourself.

I want to ask you a little favour; the next time you find yourself in a polling booth, I want you to be certain about the reasons why you are voting Conservative. And when you have – just text me the letters that are applicable.

Was it:

A. You closed your eyes and just ticked any box? Maybe your hand slipped. Two wrongs don't make a right. In this context they kind of do. A tick today can erase tomorrow.

Or:

B. To you they were the safe option. The middle road. Liberal left can seem so progressive they leave people behind, and the far right – well, they believe you can have day without night. The sun without the moon, air without oxygen. And so Conservative seemed the safest bet.

Or was it:

C. They seemed aspirational – because who wants to grow up a poor kid into an even poorer adult? I certainly don't. But having wealth shouldn't deprive others of their humanity. Did you hope, if you voted for them, that one day you'd be welcome into wealthy open arms?

Or:

D. Have your family always voted for them, so you had to? You couldn't be the odd one out. Well I know for a fact that's not true. We'll just say that one's not applicable.

Or:

E. You agree with their policies (however hollow, shallow, well-meaning or principled). You agree with their logic however fantastical. What did you agree with that they promised to do, that you could overlook all the other...shit?

Or:

This one...

   Pause.

F. I have to ask. Do you fundamentally believe that some lives are worth more than others? And that should be reflected in one's quality of life? That the wealthy can drag the poor out of poverty. 'If only everyone just worked harder, they would see that hard work is always rewarded.'

Or:

G. None of the above. Surprise me. Tell me a story.

I'm not asking you to go back in time, I'm telling you to look toward the next three years with this government because switching off isn't an option. I know living on this planet is tough, no, that's not the word. I think there was a word that no one remembers, that accurately describes the deep struggle of what it means to be a living human.

But I think one of the keys to coping with that struggle, is being each other's keeper... we used to be good at that. But presently, we are being hounded, vilified, worked to oblivion, stressed to death. To the point we can't look after ourselves let alone think about the people below us. But the thing is, they exist, those people have always existed. There is always someone below you even when you hit rock bottom and that responsibility never waivers. I still want to be your keeper but you have to step up to being mine.

Otherwise...

Sighs deeply.

When the clouds of the Apocalypse rumble
And society's cracks start to crumble
And it's finally time to eat the rich
Being from ends ain't gonna save you bitch!

Fold letter away. Thank you!

Exit to Rihanna's 'Bitch Better Have My Money'.

MFI is a bionic playwright and screenwriter from London.

NOTE: I flow in a particular way and this has been written at 140. In terms of how I read it myself, each line is the start of a new bar tempo-wise too, so basically each line is a bar. Feel free to read it at half the pace, or whatever fits and feels comfortable for you. The BPM is 63/126. Feel free to add/remove words as you see fit to make it flow better/in your own sway when you perform the lyrics. Anything that's written in italics isn't to be read out loud, it's just for you.

> *The track intro is one minute long. You can signal to the DJ to bring it in here.*
>
> *Feel free to introduce yourself to the audience.*

What you're about to hear is a rhythmic rendition of a letter from a White Male (▓▓▓) to his Black best friend (Jammz) which will be followed by his response.

Before reading the first letter, the writer would like all the Black members of the audience to come to the front and to take up space – see if there are any issues here which you can identify within your friendships with white people. I hope that we can create more dialogue around the things which are left unsaid about white privilege.

Please encourage the audience to adjust if they need it, and start when you're ready.

This is ███'s Letter to Jammz.

Dear Jam… What's Good? How's Mum? Long Time…
I know we ain't talked for a bit and it's Feeling like
we ain't got strong ties… We just stopped talking
abruptly I Wonder if these things cross your mind…
Either way though I've just been here Pondering cos
it's definitely been on mine… Back when we were
young we used to kick Ball, we were out on the road
from nine, Nowadays I text and can't hear back like to
Say I can't see you online, But I know where the
problem arose and I Know what you think – you've
got the wrong guy You keep saying that I'm not
aware of my Privilege – I already know, I'm WHITE…

You say I've got problems when it comes to Race I
really don't think it's that, I Used to get cussed by the
black kids like 'There goes the white boy who thinks
he's black' You said that I tried too hard, and I Asked
you 'What made you think it's that?' … You laughed
calmly and told me there's more to Fitting in than
wearing rings and caps, I responded and told you I'll do
it if it Means that I'm not getting kicked and slapped; It
weren't an issue of race – I tried to blend In so I didn't
get my tings dem wrapped; Growing up I had to fend for
myself and I Couldn't learn none of these things from
Dad!? He didn't wanna teach his Kids when I went
through Changes I learnt from the kings of Rap

Fitting in was something I did to sur–vive cos
back then was desperate days; But as we got
older and grew further a–part we both went
our separate ways... I know you applied to the
same Uni as Me but they never accepted J
and After; it was like you didn't wanna talk
too Much – your dreams had been kept at
bay, A part of me felt like you disliked Me cos
you couldn't accept your fate; You tried
saying my Uni rejected You cos they don't
respect your race; That's ridiculous – We're
living in the twenty-first century now no way could
the Reason that you got rejected be because
of Racism in any form or shape...

I refused to believe it... But you told me to Leave it,
so that's what I did... The years went by and we
were talking Less than we were when we were just
kids; Perspective changed as soon as I left the
borough where I once lived I weren't trying to fit into
anything like I was once when I was a kid... My new
circle of friends just like me for Me and this time of
my life was bliss... But don't get it twisted I've never
for–gotten who I am, and it is what it is... A white boy
from the endz who made it out Safely, can't you be
proud of my wins... Like Em said – if you had one
chance, would you Capture It, or let it slip?...

DJ will pull the track back and restart the instrumental.

Now you're about to hear Jammz's response to ▮▮▮ – for this
part the writer would like all white members of the audience to

come to the front, historically you tend to take up space here, but I really need you to hear this. Please step forward.

Please wait for the audience to readjust before beginning. Encourage them if they need it.

This is Jammz's response to ███.

███... What's Good; She's Fine... Long Time...
The reason we ain't talked for a bit is because; You
and I don't see through the same eyes; I tried to
explain as a teen but you Couldn't see and you
didn't wanna take time We both grew up in the
same area But it don't mean we've had the same
lives I can't front and act like I don't miss Football
outside on a late night; But even back then I was
way more aware of how it is when you ain't white...
Privilege is privilege and if you can't See that then
clearly something ain't right... And if you don't
know then educate your–self – back then you
would never make time

I said you had problems when it came to Race cos I really
think you did – You Said you got called the white boy who
thought he was Black – do you think that makes you big?
Did you think that made you sick? It made me feel sick –
you just did it to make yourself fit...
it's almost like being Black's some kinda
Accessory you just used for the win... I was
never unfair back when we were Younger – I
tried to take you in but You were so ignorant to
what your privilege Was, I just wanted to make
you think... You're lucky if you can change your
appea–rance to stop people taking things...

Cos when the situation's over you could go
Home and experience gracious things...

The notion of choosing when to be Black is quite
an outrageous thing I'm black when I'm here, black
when I go home So how can you start simulating
things... He's right – when I got turned down from
Uni, I never rated him, cos Even though we both
came from the same path My outcome weren't the
same as his;

When I voiced my opinion you tried to Say no
issues of race exist, if that's the case you tell me
why I never got Picked – I had the same grades
as his! You can't tell me that you're not privileged
after that, that's just a blatant diss; And if you
can't see that now then I Have to wonder, what is
it you take from this?

Notice how you said when you got older you didn't have
to keep on tryna fit in... Young white boy made it out of
the hood And you wanna know why I ain't happy for the
win... You can be like us when it suits you un–til it's time
to put your mask in the bin; for me it's not like that – I
play the cards I was dealt I can't change the tone of my
skin... It's like we're both in a race but you Got the ability
to swap the car that you're in; Meanwhile I've gotta use
what I have and just Fight through from the back half of
the grid... I don't hate you... I just want you to be a–ware
of the privileged path on which you've skipped... It's like
when you do it it's cool, but When I do it it's a cardinal
sin... And one more

Thing – I noticed how you referenced Eminem in
your letter, Kinda I–ronic, using that quote
doesn't make what you did any better, See I
know a Thousand rappers in the hood who are
just as witty and just as clever, but don't have
Privileges like you both, and won't see his Level
of success ever... Do the math...

Jammz is a grime MC, record producer and the founder of the record label I
Am Grime. His free EP *Hit Then Run* became a cult classic: the title track was
playlisted on BBC 1Xtra and was Noisey's #3 Grime track of 2015. Jammz has
been supported heavily by Fader, Noisey, FACT, GQ, Mixmag, SBTV, MTV, and
featured on the front cover of the *Observer Music*'s British MCs special.

MIKA ONYX JOHNSON

Dear So-Called Allies,

Listen, before we get started, I just wanna say – I see you and I know you get a lot of the bullshit; I know people are out here trying you every day in their own micro way; I call them people ninjas cuz everything is so low-key and hard to detect (in their eyes anyways – we've clocked their shit from early). But anyway there's a few things I wanna talk to you about that you'll never experience, some things you'll know all too well, but I'm just trying to make my chest feel a little lighter and I'm hoping you can recognise where there's work still to be done.

Pride was a protest so they say
A fight
A riot for change
Noise and violence

ACAB
All cops are bastards
Batons and silence

New York, Manhattan, Stonewall, 1969

Gay liberation
Fedz instigate
Lives on the line
And herstories made

Obviously I wasn't there and it's likely you weren't either, but I've heard and read about the birthplace of 'Pride'. I sat in the Stonewall Inn earlier this year, I drank overpriced beer, trust me they make mad money in there – two-drink minimum they told me, after I'd ordered my first drink of course – for a hot sec I was shook, batty all tense cotched on this historical soaked barstool. I see you there you don't flinch when them facts come your way you're happy to oblige to them prices no problem, I scanned the bar, a womxn sat next to me

white
bartender
white
gay man
white
more tourists…yes I'm a tourist but they were
white
white
white

Once I'd recovered from shock from the overpriced beer I thought about what this iconic landmark might mean to me and other people in the LGBTQ+ community, and what this history has created for my existence, for the life I live today – what was mad though was that I never saw any mention of Marsha P. Johnson or Sylvia Rivera. I'm assuming you know who they are?

Anyway – I wondered if their names and faces had been carved into the walls behind the Stonewall novelty tees for sale, or if their photos were just lost amongst all the white punters' bodies blocking the walls; I wondered if there were any other trans people inside the bar; and as I took my final extortionate sip of beer, I hoped that I might catch a glimpse of a black or brown face – maybe they were out of sight? Amongst the shadows, also analysing the overwhelming whiteness, being pissed off at the two-drink minimum trap and wondering WTF they were doing in there.

I leave the bar dazed and confused, I swagger across the road to the other side and spy the many many rainbow flags waving in the breeze... I lie it was hot as fuck, there weren't no breeze. I collect each colour in my mind, red orange yellow, green blue purple, and try to recall the meaning of this now-cultural capital flag, *your* flag.

Pride was a protest so they say
A fight
A riot for change
Noise and violence

ACAB
All cops are bastards
Batons and silence

New York, Manhattan, Stonewall, 1969

Gay liberation
Fedz instigate
Lives on the line
And herstories made

Remember that time at *your* pub?

Remember, I'd been avoiding you, I knew that night wouldn't really be my vibe, but I made an appearance cuz I didn't wanna be dry and I'd already had a couple drinks during the day, so I thought – yeah I'll roll out again. I spy the many many rainbow flags, bunting – next to the rainbow hangs a Great British flag, side by side, many of them, just attached to the exterior of the pub, they wave in the night breeze. Now you're gonna call me dramatic and wrong no doubt but don't you think there's something a bit off about that?

Feels exclusive, feels a tad bit insidious, feels a bit *I heart Boris*, no? Cuz every time I see that flag it makes my skin crawl slightly and my mind time-travel, and all that generational trauma seems to seep its way to my fingertips. I accidentally picture things and people and then… You know that weird feeling you get when you walk into a space and no one looks like you? And you just know what the vibe's gonna be but you stay anyway cuz you don't wanna be that guy, do you get me?

Anyway – you're sitting by the bar, the pub's obviously been there for a minute, it's old school, the gays and the hets are in their element here, probably a lot of regulars. I'm a couple drinks in, I've been 'social smoking', and suddenly I'm busting, so I stroll back into the now-bustling pub, the Great British flags still lurking over my shoulder – I think Kylie Minogue is playing, of course she is – anyways – I look at you… You look back… I make my way to the ladies' toilet, as it's labelled, it's one cubicle and I've just seen two people go in there and I assume they're mash up, probably having a heart-to-heart alongside a key of coke perhaps, whatever, I ain't waiting, so I head for the men's toilet now, as it's labelled, and that's when your friends holla at your boi –

'Oi where are you going, the ladies' is down there, that ain't your toilet'

I CBA with the chat, also like I said before labour ain't free, so I one-eighty and make my way back down to the ladies' toilet, as it's labelled – this is your castle, you're king here, I can feel your eyes on me, yes I'm sexy, the old queen that owns this place is bopping about, bunting above my head, rainbow flag, Great British flag, I heart Boris, wanna leave, don't wanna be that guy, transphobic, don't wanna cause a fuss so I swallow the spit that contained the words I wanted to let rip,
would've sounded something like

'Listen, I'll use whatever toilet I want to, mind your damn business and this pub smells like piss anyways'

But like I said I don't wanna be that guy, so I turn to look at *you* and I wonder if it's cosy from where you're sitting? Perched on that fence I see you bystanding

I just want you to know your silence is as loud as any insult

I just want you to know your silence slaps harder than any bare hand stinging silence blaring ringing in my ears

I just want you to know if you saw it take place
you heard every word
felt the energy
felt the anxiety
saw my body twitch,
then your proximity
was close to where the event took place,
eyes raised over half-pints of IPA
muttering mumbling, cat got your tongue
later you'll be stumbling

over words you didn't say
anyway
you didn't tell me I couldn't use them toilets
in fact *you* did absolutely nothing at all

Pride was a protest so they say
A fight
A riot for change
Noise and violence

ACAB
All cops are bastards
Batons and silence

New York, Manhattan, Stonewall, 1969

Gay liberation
Fedz instigate
Lives on the line
And herstories made

Remember at the start when I said I see you, and that there's a few things you will know too well?

Well.

You put your hand in my hair but it's *you* innit so I think that's okay, but for real, did Solange teach you nothing?

I mean you took up all the space at Lovebox to see her perform did you not?

'FOR US THIS SHIT IS FOR US'

You love black music, your ears crave more than that top-forty beige, I get it, but you can't really hear it can you?
All you do is listen

There have been several occasions where I've gone to see a black artist perform, I'm five-foot-four so standing at venues is always a bit of a bitch for me, and I've had you walk in front of me and block my view – I've tapped your shoulder and asked politely for you to shift, your eyes rolling, and you move maybe half an inch, when in reality that music, black music, those lyrics ain't for you. But that's entitlement, right?

I remember being at several supposedly inclusive events for queers and then leaving feeling violated, not just by them overplayed pop anthems, but by your entitlement, by your unwanted performance of 'wokeness', your need to express your anger towards society, how racism is shitty and how you wanna see more queer POC performing at big queer events – I nod and hum and make no eye contact and you still continue to flap your gums. We have since laid the word 'woke' to rest, it lives no more, mostly because you all decided you'd use it for yourselves and kill it dead. And the thing is most events such as Pride aren't inclusive, if they were we black and brown queers wouldn't have to create our own spaces, and the majority of the time you all still feel so entitled that you turn up to our events anyway, claiming you're an ally, but in actual fact it's an infiltration of space that isn't for you. Can we not have something that belongs to us?

You know how black folks are cultural capital, right?

How everyone loves our culture but doesn't love us, and just cuz you're gay and love Beyoncé you think you can claim language that don't belong to you… I'm sorry, I think I'm still recovering from *RuPaul's Drag Race UK* and it's all pouring out of me now. Did you enjoy it? You and the cis-hets, glitter party beside the TV?

I'm watching and I'm confused, I'm sighing, I'm kissing my teeth, I'm laughing, I'm laughing cuz I think that's my body's way of dealing with frustration, I speak to the TV, I wonder why Baga Chipz is wearing a turban and I'm offended by his disrespectful performance of Amy Winehouse. I ask the TV, 'WHERE ARE ALL THE BLACK PEOPLE?'

Met Gala 2019. You saw them pictures right? I know you did, Billy Porter, Indya Moore, Janet Mock, MJ Rodriguez. Lena Waithe wears a pin-striped double-breasted Pyer Moss suit with the words 'Black Drag Queens Invented Camp'. Say no more – I'm not saying you can't love drag, or perform in drag if you ain't black, before you go there, of course I ain't – but I feel like there's a lack of awareness, I feel like black and brown people ain't celebrated enough in our community – there's this idea that because you're gay and at some point in our history it was illegal for you to exist, for you to love who you wanted publicly, you couldn't possibly be that privileged – but you're still white and a man, you don't walk into queer spaces and think 'is this for me?' even when you see rainbow flags all over the place. We had to create our own events, our own spaces to validate our existence, our experiences – when I see a rainbow flag on an establishment that don't mean safe space to me – that still feels like uncertainty.

Pride was a protest so they say
A fight
A riot for change
Noise and violence

ACAB
All cops are bastards
Batons and silence

New York, Manhattan, Stonewall, 1969

Gay liberation
Fedz instigate
Lives on the line
And herstories mad

Black womxn are not your accessory, they are not your Beyoncé, Rihanna or Cardi B, and queer people ain't either. There was no invitation for you to touch my body or my hair, stop snapping your fingers, stop saying *YASSSSSSSS* and calling black womxn *GURL*. Microaggressions are racism, covert and ninja in tone – you are not exempt – see, see this labour I'm doing for free now?

Look, I don't hate you. I got love for you. But I also wanna talk about your misogyny, I think it's important, I think a lot about the level of respect you have for womxn and AFAB people, maybe you need to unpack your shit, you say you're an ally, you've boarded that ship, sailing – but when them waves get rough, choppy, things are getting bumpy, are you gonna be an anchor?

When I tell you my pronouns are they/them and you continue to call me 'girl' or 'she' and I let it ride, inside it's a real pain – sometimes I can't bring myself to correct you on the spot cuz I don't wanna make you feel bad, funny that innit?

I don't wanna make *you* feel bad – and yes, I see your Twitter profile and your Insta bio with your pronouns added as well, but that means nothing to me if you aren't actually doing any work beyond an internet facade my friend – yeah, yeah, you watched both seasons of *Pose* and bought tickets to a trans artist's show, but what are you actually doing?

You lot wanna consume our culture for entertainment to make yourselves feel better – you're doing your part, you might think, but how many of you actually start conversations with your family? Or at work? Or on the tube when someone is experiencing violence?

I often hear 'liberal' people complaining about non-binary identities and trans issues in general, whether that's on TV or in my physical presence. The idea of someone correcting *you* on pronouns is alarming, or gendered language changing throughout businesses or schools is a step too far, but if someone misgenders your French bulldog it's another story. You care more about someone eating a cow than the rights of human beings.

Sometimes I've seen how you have this tendency to talk down to me, to dismiss my wishes and my presence – misogyny lives in all of us, it's this patriarchal society we live in after all – but I feel like in these moments I see your entitlement and privilege – you aren't even aware cuz you live in it, it is you. We've been out, in a group and you've told me about an incident of racism and how you should've said something but you didn't, instead you just tell me how you should've. Stop, just stop talking, I don't wanna know. If you're gonna bystand, bystand – you don't tell a black person all the ways you wish you hadn't.

Pride was a protest so they say
A fight
A riot for change
Noise and violence

ACAB
All cops are bastards
Batons and silence

New York, Manhattan, Stonewall, 1969

Gay liberation
Fedz instigate
Lives on the line
And herstories made

Remember that time I'd just moved to London and a good friend of mine let me stay on her sofa for a few months until I found my feet? She was away that weekend and I'd been to see a show at Soho – a drag king show actually, I was on a nice likkle high. I came back to the flat and you were there, drinking at the table with my friend's cousin, him gay also but black, light-skinned like me; you were Irish, you talked to me about how hard that was for you, living there being catholic and gay and having to leave home. I listened, I was invested in this mostly one-sided conversation. My friend was away that weekend, like I said, so I felt a little outta place in that moment – sometimes when you enter a space that feels familiar it can suddenly feel unfamiliar when a new presence is present. Sure I'd been sleeping on that sofa but something in my body was tingling, like restless legs or the start of calf cramps. I had a glass of wine with you and then music started playing – it was house I think – you took a hula hoop that didn't belong to you, you began to wiggle your teeny tiny hips, and surprisingly that hoop found some kinda off-beat rhythm, if you could call it that – think Miley Cyrus combined with twerk – anyways I smiled, I was feeling overly cautious though cuz you were knocking into the blinds and the sofa – again not your yard – anyways I said:

'You have to work on your rhythm'
cuz you couldn't keep the hoop in motion, then you said

'Oh shut up, you're not even English'
I can't remember what I said in that moment, honestly, but I think I just laughed it off, especially after my friend's cousin said something passive like
'Oh none of us are English'

Trying to move on from the awkward situation before things got any worse, then you carried on hooping until you couldn't be arsed anymore.

Pride was a protest so they say
A fight
A riot for change
Noise and violence

ACAB
All cops are bastards
Batons and silence

New York, Manhattan, Stonewall, 1969

Gay liberation
Fedz instigate
Lives on the line
And herstories made

I don't like Pride, I think you know why.
I think I've made it obvious by this point.
I said never again after Brighton Pride 2018, and that took some serious motivation for me to even get there. I say thank God for Black Pride, I say thank God for visibility and for beautiful black and brown queers.

Like I said before – I don't hate you, I got a lot of love in my heart – I just think sometimes you need to check yourself, you need to understand that everything doesn't belong to you and standing on the sidelines isn't helping anyone. Don't make noise when we have black and PoC-only queer events – you know why we're doing this. I just think that it's important that queer herstory is depicted properly; that black and brown queers are given that recognition and that thanks.

When you're at your next Pride event, or watching *RuPaul* and sprinkling that glitter, just remember the names of the trans women of colour that paved the way.

Pride was a protest so they say
A fight
A riot for change
Noise and violence

ACAB
All cops are bastards
Batons and silence

New York, Manhattan, Stonewall, 1969

Gay liberation
Fedz instigate
Lives on the line
And herstories made

I send this letter with love,

Mika

Mika Onyx Johnson is an actor, writer and performance artist. Recent writing credits include *Pink Lemonade* (The Queer House/HighTide, 2019).

JASMINE LEE-JONES

To Erin

Hey
It's been a while since I saw you last
In fact, I think the last time might have been five months ago
I was on the train with a friend and I saw you sitting a few seats
down with your headphones in
I pretended not to see you
Watched you twiddle the cord between your iPhone and ears
And watched you peer
Out of the window.
I know you saw me or at least I'm pretty sure
Because I saw you
So maybe you were pretending not to see me too.

It's funny that
Because six years before
In secondary
we walked home together every day
Do you remember?
Trawling through Church Street at quarter past three

Treading our much-trodden path before separating shortly
after the A10?

We discovered we walked
(or at least could walk) the same way home in our first two days
of year seven
Discovered our paths to and away were more or less the same.

I thought of you recently – well I didn't start thinking of you but I
remembered a feeling I felt around you then I remembered you –
let me explain.
I was doing a post-show Q and A
And I was sat next to another playwright – who is also con-
veniently called Erin –
And two other women who were chairing the panel about both
of our plays.
One of the women chairing commented that our plays both
had queer women in them
And the other playwright who happened to have your name
mentioned that the references to
queer sex in her play 'came directly from experience'
The audience sniggered
and then there was this silence.

.

.

.

.

My silence.
I didn't say anything.

Nothing about how I knew what my character Kara was going through
How I had dug deep
Burrowed into myself
To characterise her
To tell the truth about what it is to live a lie
To be stuck in a closet constantly
Spend long hours crying
Agonising over it
Whilst simultaneously longing
Pining to have my desires fulfilled
Then kind of coming out?
Only to keep coming out over and over again because no one ever ever ever expects you to be anything but straight.

Instead
I swallowed the sharp-edged truth
Sword-like
Stabbed my insides
Vital organs
Lungs
once again
Suspended breath.

This puncturing
This blood
This bruise
This dull sensation
Was a familiar echo-ache
A pain
A silence
Familiar feeling I felt around you.

When we walked home together
Silence was a regular occurence
Sometimes the silences were comfortable
Other times well they were the other kind.
Pregnant with subtext
Subliminal messages
Wonder
Longing.

You were my first grown-up friend
And by that I mean
Grown-up as in going to grown-up secondary school
Our friendship came as a sort of surprise
At least to me
We were an unlikely pair
I was lanky
Lithe
Awkward
With a headful of canerows.
You were tomboyish
A football fanatic
Wore stiff grey starched school trousers
With your shoulder-length brown hair that acted as a curtain
over the emerald of your eyes
And you were well
White.

I mean not that I hadn't had or would have white friends
I mean there was Claudine and Ava in primary but we weren't
close friends or at least didn't stay close consistently.
The friends I held to my bosom
Shared secrets with
Confided crushes in

Even from primary
Were all black
And well I have always had
And still do
a complicated relationship with
– or should I say to? –
white women.

It's a complicated mix of disdain, jealousy and even fascination
See you all – I speak generally now –
Are everywhere
Magazines
Billboards
Blockbusters
You name it
You're there
And even as a child, when I saw myself it wasn't a knotty haired
broad-nosed full-lipped
reflection that met me in the mirror
it was something profoundly more sanitised
Diluted even
I can remember
Standing in Shabas beauty supply
surrounded by a ten-foot sea of hair dyes
Relaxers
No-lye
Watching the boxes plastered with budget Beyonce prototypes
Black women that seemed to be emulating white women
Or at least some ancient great white ocean that equalled beauty.
Regardless of the aforementioned rage
Our friendship somehow managed to be sweet
And the perfect kind of sweet

Like spiced bun
You know how it carries on
With that touch of the savoury so it's not too saccharine
I mean
after all
You weren't exactly like the rest
With your androgynous swagger
Your whip-smart sarcasm
Your humour
Your kind and thoughtful ear
You were smarter
Studious-like.
We were both bookish
Nerds
And unashamed of the fact.
We could match each other with our wit
We kinda thought we were both the shit
Prided ourselves on our intelligence
In a way that most girls
That age
Black or white
Just don't.

It's now time for me to apologise. And after the aforementioned you must understand I don't take apologising to white women – moreover white people – lightly. But I definitely need to apologise to you. I also think you should too but for now it's my turn. This might sound weird suggesting we apologise to each other after all these years but let me re-jig your memory.

Do you remember that three weeks in year seven when I started to ignore you? Air you on our long walks home? Abandon you when you went to go and get chips? Went the ridiculously long way home on the A10 which took twice as long for no apparent reason? You might have thought it was because I wanted to hang with the cool kids. You know people that were actually popular.

It wasn't.

You see a few nights before I started acting weird I'd had a dream. You were in it.

For some reason you were standing in my grandmother's doorway with a football in tow
As you do
Staring at me
Your eyes somewhere between their green and blue
And something stirred inside of me.
Even back then I knew exactly what it meant
And when I woke up I wasn't immediately scared
No.
I wasn't scared until I saw you in person the next day
And the feelings hadn't quite gone away
I was confused
And I started to act weird around you.

I remember being paired with you during a drama class by miss during that weird couple of weeks
And I must have barely hid my frown
Because all I remember you saying is
'Why don't you like me anymore?'
Your eyes so serious
I acted like you were acting crazy
But deep inside an ancient fear grew in me
Which had been growing
Had been there
since I'd been born.

I'd always assumed
These feelings:
Longing for the flesh of another woman
Wanting to press my body against a body like my own
Were something every woman experienced
Didn't associate them with being part of a six-letter alphabet
Or seven-lettered rainbow
I just thought it was the way all girls were
But I was wrong.

Somehow – and I can't actually remember how – we recovered
from that three-week itch
I think I just managed to wrestle, repress the feeling again
So we started anew
became known as a terrible twosome
You were a self-proclaimed goody two shoes
But also somehow managed to get away with a healthy dose of
tongue and cheek
You were a character
Popular with teachers
And most students
I say most because at times you were a sarky bitch and you
knew it
You teased me when I didn't know the name of which famous
actor Sam Taylor-Wood was married to
and frowned when I couldn't remember who'd won the best
actress Oscar in 2002.

On the way home we'd share chips from the shop for a pound
a piece
You'd grimace when I'd try and offer you small change in
exchange for a handful.
We got put on all the gifted and talented schemes together

You let me be nerdy
A blerd
Before I even knew what that was
You made me think my intelligence was cool just by being
unashamed of yours
Taught me it was okay to show up to school just how I wanted
That I didn't need to be pristinely put together aesthetically
That I could just be.

But even though those weird three weeks passed
The monster-ache of longing and lust
still loomed large
I managed to feed it with the sweat and secretions of videos on
RedTube and PornHub
Lust writhed
Wriggled
Forced me into cold sweats
Caterpillar country
In mornings
Evenings
And afternoons
Forced me to wrestle with myself in my bedroom
I'd cry and pray to God that this really was just a phase
I gripped my duvet in delusion-confusion
A perfectly balanced hyphenated mix
I just couldn't understand how it was abnormal
How other women's insides didn't twitch when they saw a
woman's curves cross their paths
And I was confused
Cos wasn't there Jonathan in primary I crushed on hard
fancied all the way consecutively from year two to year five
until he moved to the seaside?

Though there hadn't really been any in secondary
Male crushes that is
Or crushes of any kind
No one I took a fancy to
Except maybe a bit you.
And in puberty boys had
Broadened
Become big
Haired
Whilst women were still soft
Docile
Cushion-y
A place where my head could rest.

I'd lie there in my bed
Fingers between my legs
Imagining head
Finger
Mouth
Touch.
Lust and other words live shrouded in secret in the world wide
web portal between my thumbs
And inside a part of me wanted to run.

It's funny
because people always suspected you not me
Smelt the dyke on you
Like a cheap perfume
In between your after-school extracurriculars
The wide-legged grey of your school trousers
The sharp, straight line of your hair
You were an easy target.
When you came into school with a skirt

For the first time in year eight
The whole school gasped
Erin in a skirt
And inside part of me laughed
Because even then I knew you were being tied down strangled
to constraints that were also secretly strangling me.
Albeit less openly.

Our political differences were difficult at times
And we would disagree, argue.
All the same, I felt protected by you
When my hair broke off at twelve after years of abuse at the
hands of a store-bought texturiser
I decided I wanted to rock the natural look™ before rocking
the natural look™ was a thing.

You supported me
Told me when my hair stuck up in class out of my two french
braids so that I could ward off
the taunts and inevitable onslaught
From our unkind peers
And you literally stood by me
When *black* hands (and not white – those would come too
eventually) fingered my fro on the
first day of term when I decided to come in rocking an afropuff
which didn't meet the
scrupulous baby-hairs-ecostyled-with-a-toothbrush standards
of the lighties
And their darker, mouthy canerowed compatriots
I remember Mariame towering over me
Her voice like a harbinger
Herald of hell to come
'It will break if you leave it out like that you know'

She boomed as I watched the microbraids on her hairline drag
her hair back to where it came from.

Even then before we were all initiated into wokedom
Before it became cool, fashionable for white people to want be woke
You knew not to broach the hair subject with me or
Comment on which of my many many hair experiments was
your fave.
Unlike many of your white and black counterparts
You never once came an inch close to my scalp with your words
or your hands
You just seemed to understand.

You were an ally before it was cool
Brave in ways even in adulthood I see white women squirm
and cease to be
supported me when the other black girls tried to disauthenticate
my blackness
When that same girl
Mariame
Between the scoffs and giggles of her peers asked me in the
school changing room if I could
dutty wine before PE
You said confidently
'Yeah, she can I've seen her'
Without even a blink
Even though you definitely hadn't.

Race was difficult for me
Although I was friendly with the black girls across the classes
I wasn't quite considered one of them
Not in their gang
I was the last to find out their secrets

Who was going out with who
I never had a pair of kickers
And I also never had the right hairdo.

There were the self-proclaimed 'lighties' in our English class for
whom being light-skinned
Seemed to be a brand
A badge they wore proudly
with swollen excessive pride
Like tear drops under their eyes
They carried it confident and high
With their rolled-up skirts and their short fat ties
Secretly I longed to be one of them
Well not one of them
But considered as beautiful by other people
As beautiful as sometimes I saw myself in the mirror on the
off-glance
As beautiful as when one of the lighties considered me when she –
With her edges dripping with gel
And her ponytail frizzed and frayed to high heaven
Pimples purpling through on her cheeks
Looked at me the right way one sunny day
And said
'Jasmine you're actually so beautiful'
And another replied
'I know if she just let me do her weave!'

You see I couldn't agree to force myself into a cookie cutter
category based on the shade and colour of my skin
It's just not where I wanted to be.

Eventually we managed to find ourselves our own group anyway
Found ourselves sitting comfortably alongside a group of more outliers
Oddballs
Crazies
The kids who dragged twigs against school gates to make percussive music
At break
The yutes who made up satirical sketches in our spare time
Worthy of Saturday Night Live.
We were a patchwork of colours and heights and sizes
You loved the movie The Breakfast Club and I imagined we were like them except from endz.
I finally felt at home
Dysfunctional and proud
Like I could be pretty much whoever I wanted to be
And finally I started to feel free
And that included being weird
And strange
But
For some reason even in this offshoot branch of idiotic idiosyncratics
The queer thing still wasn't quite cool
You and the others
Even in our group of oddballs
Used the label
Lesbian
Gay
Like it was an insult regularly
Spoke those identities and turned them into slurs
And this is why I want an apology.

When those jokes
Words were tossed around in tandem
Boomeranged this way and that
I want you to know I was the one getting hit
Repeatedly
Bleeding
And I'd just sit there stock silent
Feeling the hit from the inside.
You see I thought my silence would protect me
And it would take me years for Audre to teach me it wouldn't.
Years before crenshaw called out to me
Teaching me how to spell intersectionality
Before baldwin bowled me over
Before hemphill hailed me a cab home
Yes before I discovered Giovanni and his room I was stuck in
my own.

Again I felt like an anomaly
Like a square in a round hole
Odd
Weird
Trying to fit myself into something I wasn't
And not only that but I was swallowing myself whole
That sharp as fuck sword was near skewering me in two
And I did not know what to do.

At sixteen I applied to go to a vocational college
And got in
It would be arty
And there might be more kids like me
In more ways than one.

In year eleven things got weird between us, again
I threw myself into our exams
Locking myself away after school and at weekends.
Spending long evenings and weekends alone with only the company of textbooks and BBC Bitesize
They became my most loyal friends
I guess work was something I could control
And well
My body
My desires
Just weren't.

You drifted into yet another group of kids
Forged another identity with them
And I formed an island of self
Marooned myself there
We left each other without punctuation mark
So the end smelt sour
Stank of bitterness
Especially on my part
Jealousy strangled me when we jointly opened our envelopes come results day

I had locked myself in my room every day for months on end
trapped by an unhealthy desire for excellence
Believing as a young, intelligent black woman being academically exceptional was my only source of worth and respectability.
You, on the other hand, had just skirted along
Naturally intelligent
Barely revising
And confident about it too (I always envied that about you)
I did swimmingly in my exams

Getting nothing below an A
But when I found out that miraculously you had somehow managed to get four more A stars than me
And ten points higher in our performance exam
My heart sank
All I wanted to be was the best actress in the world and I'd managed to get a B
In performance
Which I made up for in the writing assessment
But still
It felt like a punch to the gut for a young Meryl Streep wannabe
Perhaps this was my first experience of white girls seeming to put half the effort in and somehow doing twice as well
Maybe it was just your ease
Maybe that was the key to it after all
I always envied your confidence
It was like a tease
When you walked into the room
You knew what you were speaking about and why
Knew you deserved to be there
You didn't shrink.
You were my first acquaintance with the confidence which sometimes borderlined entitlement which I tended to see uniquely with white women
I mean I guess I should thank you for that
It meant
Means I'm not so surprised in life when I see white women demand things like gender parity with a far less polite, no fucks tone than me and be treated by everyone – especially men, white and black – with more respect and less severity.
I mean, at least in the future when I encountered it
I had a way of dealing with it

Contextualising it
After all, I'd seen it a bit before
With you.
This isn't meant to sound bitter.
It's just true.

Even though we left each other literally
I met versions of you everywhere
Felt echoes of you throughout the years.

At college there was Elisa
Blonde
Bright-eyed
Who I once had a long debate with about white privilege and
white beauty standards
Over the oak table in the art rooms
She was hard to get on side
But once she was fuck was she an ally.
She spoke up against structural injustices and hypocrises.
And after Ferguson, marched into the headteachers office with
me and suggested we form a school rally
Against police brutality.
She cradled me when I complained about my strength and
directness as a black-girl-becoming-a-black-woman always
being conflated with manliness
Masculinity
She understood intersectionality.

Then there was Emilia
We met at drama school
And I always knew she'd be cool
In first year she called out the way the teachers relied on the
gender binary

To split us into groups
Was the first to call out in person to a teacher's face (even before me) the banality
Of our totally white, cis, male, able-bodied curriculum.
She wasn't afraid to call out an academic ecology that took too long to change.
I confided in her and she confided in me about what we really thought about the people or
should I say pricks
Academics in positions of power
Some of whom abused it
And pretended they were on our side only to protect each other time and time again.
She clocked when people tried to call me crazy and nipped it in the proverbial and literal bud
Told gaslighters – and there were many – to grow the fuck up.
She called bullshit when the school refused to give me my degree
If I left early
To write my play
Whilst letting four others leave for opportunities and not treating them the same.
And she was the only, only person to back me
When I politely, indiscriminately suggested positive discrimination and employing more
teachers of colour was not tantamount to a decline in our training's quality
and was consequently screamed at in front of the whole school and all of the all-white faculty
By a senior member of staff
Whilst no one else including the teacher employed to 'tackle diversity'

Whatever the fuck that means
Stepped in to defend me.

So I guess this is also an acknowledgement
Love letter to all of you
White women
Who never spoke over or for me
But made the space for me to speak
To be.
Supported me in silence and in actuality
Used your privilege to protect me
Whilst not aching for a thank-you or to be deigned as my
saviour.
You all stood with me in the corners of corridors
Canteens
Crevices of the A10
Crystal Palace
Selhurst
City of London.
Here's to you
the ones I have loved and lost.
And Erin
You were the first
You set the pattern
Precedent
And all paths lead back to you.

I haven't seen you since that train ride
And I don't know how you are
Or how you identify
The last time I checked your Instagram there was no trace of
a partner
And sometimes I wonder

If I wasn't the only one swallowing swords
Doing circus feats, magic tricks
To hide who I was
I mean
There was your androgynous dress
Your no-fucks attitude
And that stare
I'll never forget the look in your eyes
When you thought I'd abandoned you
Maybe you were hiding something too…

Erin…
Are you queer?

.

.

.

You don't have to answer.
You're not obligated to.
But if you want to
I'm here, even after all these years
and if you are
If you are like me
I hope you know there are spaces for us
Where we don't exist on the periphery
Parties
Places
Books for us too, literature, languages, litanies, with experiences
like our own.
And even if you aren't…queer.
I want to let you know

It has got better for me.
Sometimes it's still confusing but better:
Over the years, I've found refuge in the BBZs
Been coronated in pussy palaces
Trailed long paths home through hackney wick
Laughed until I cried with chums for life on the jubilee line
And I'm here.
I'm twenty-one now......
I'm still not out to my parents
Well they know
But I've never said it
It still feels too hard for me.
I guess it's proof the silent shame is still seeping through
somewhere. –

Two weeks after that panel. I had lunch with the other Erin.
I looked at her and recognised something I saw in you
And Elisa
And Emilia
Bravery
Strength
That we might become friends.
We were talking about me going to New York
Do you remember how I always said I wanted to go?
I told her I'd been looking at the best places to visit and found
this list on Autostraddle called
'Queer Girls Guide to NYC'.
She looked at me a little funny
And then replied,
'Are you... I mean I thought you might be, your play it read as
being written by a...but in the
Q and A when you didn't say...'

Funny that.
How silences tend to speak volumes
How even when I'm hiding
Abstaining from spoken word
Some words on a page speak for me
Bring forth my truth.
Maybe that's why I'm a writer.

Her question hung in the air for a while
Till I replied
'Yeah, I am…queer.'

And despite sometimes still living in the silence. Being occasionally hit by the blunt edge of trauma and shame. Most of me is proud. And not just of that part of myself. But even the less pleasant memories that have moved, morphed and made me.
Us walking down church street as night hit in our kilts black and blue
Skin black and white
Kind of like an inverted moonlight.

This is all to say,
I often think of you
Maybe
Let's talk soon?

Jasmine

Jasmine Lee-Jones is a writer and performer. Her first play *seven methods of killing kylie jenner* (Royal Court Theatre, 2019) won the 2019 Alfred Fagon Award, the *Stage* Debut Award for Best Writer and the *Evening Standard* Charles Wintour Award for Most Promising Playwright.

SUHAIYMAH MANZOOR-KHAN

NOTE: The actor reading the letter must be a man of Pakistani or Bangladeshi heritage born in Britain.

This is a letter for brown boys who go out with white girls.

The writer says that I, as a brown boy, in this moment, stand in for all brown boys ever – and I am all the ones in this letter.

She would like to acknowledge that she knows this letter already sounds bitter; she knows we're trying not to roll our eyes as we are hearing this and that we're thinking, *'She's been humiliated, this is a personal vendetta she wants to play out on a stage.'*

We're thinking, *'It's almost embarrassing.'*

'What? We can't go out with white girls now?
Isn't that a bit…superficial?
Isn't that a bit reductive?
Isn't it even, I daresay, racist?
How is romantic preference something you can write a whole letter about?'

   Pause.

She says don't worry though, she anticipated that – our exasperation, our disbelief, even, our slight cringing.

But here we've got a few minutes. More than she usually gets. And this time we can't dismiss her; I can't scrunch up this paper and turn away. I can't pass her by on the street and laugh a little louder to cover it up.

Before she gets into it, she's asked, could all brown men please move to the front... Yes, now please.

I have to wait until you have.

    Wait whilst they do.

Almost a year ago, the writer of this letter was on a bus in New York City.

The night was full of that sort of quivering feeling that nights have when you're a tourist in a big city; as if the next day might never come and you might just sit on the precipice laughing forever.

A brown boy got on the bus too, or no, he must have already been on it. All she heard were the voices.

A giggling white girl – hard to miss – and then an accent that felt like home: British Asian boy, unmistakable.
A sound that rang of school,
a sound that rang of Harehills,
of Manningham,
of Whitechapel,
Southall, Alum Rock, Green Street, Tooting, Heathrow terminal three – unmistakeable, unmistakeably home.

They sat right behind her so it wasn't eavesdropping, it was just an inevitable part of the journey and they spoke loudly anyway, in that way that it was obvious that they had only just met tonight.

She knew that the brown boy – me, in this case, as the stand in for all brown boys in this moment– that I had clocked her, of course I had, it would have been impossible not to, we were the only two brown people on the bus. But I pretended I didn't, looked over her head, avoided any eye contact.

I talked animatedly to the white girl next to me
unable to hide the adulation in my voice
unable to hide the way that her eyes on me were the closest thing to being a man I had ever felt.

I'd do anything to keep those eyes on me.
Adoration meant for the types of boys they show you in films.
I'd do anything for that.

After a while the white girl asks me, '*Did you go to see the 9/11 memorial?*'

    Pause.

To be honest I wish she hadn't asked so loudly.
I say *yes* quickly and then try to touch her in some new way that might divert us back to pretending.

That might brush over this momentary relapse
might hold the surreality of the night in place just a little longer and divert us back to pretending I might be just a man.

Just a man.

Touch her in some way that might divert us back to pretending that I might be able to shed this skin,

that when she takes these clothes off me she might take off the
connotations with them.

Touch her in some way that might distract us back to pretending I
might be able to shed the marks that my face leaves on the mind,
the way my name bears connotations constructed decades
before my birth,

but

no amount of touching can trick whiteness into loving you as
if you were it.

I didn't know that yet.
Maybe I still don't.

  Pause.

She smirks and says,
'Wasn't it awkward…you know, cos…?'

  Pause.

and in what can only have been milliseconds that passed after
those words and my response; the closeness of me and her – her
with her white arm on my thigh, with my lips soon to be on
hers – was nothing compared to the closeness of me and the
brown girl sat in front of me.

Was nothing compared to the way those words were a gleaming
embarrassment.

Words that said to the bus that my pretending was obvious.
That she hadn't thought me white to start.
That I hadn't been able to transcend this skin through the
badge of her desire.

'Wasn't it awkward…you know, cos…?'

Words that embarrass me to the brown girl in front
the brown girl who I had pretended I had nothing in common
with but who I have now been chained to.
The brown girl in front who I passed by
who I always pass by and laugh a little louder while I do
hiding from the fact that if I caught her eye, if I did not laugh,
I might see in her something I wouldn't want to address;
I might see in her the parts of me I am trying to suppress.

'Wasn't it awkward…. you know, cos…?'

In the utterance of that question the brown girl I tried to drop
is tied to me
we're in the interrogation waiting room together
we're chastised in the headlines together
we're spat at in the street together
her, who I pretended was a cringeworthy connection might now
have been the only person on the bus who saw me as just a man.

Might have been the only person on the bus who saw me as
just a boy
just a familiar accent
a reminder of home
a nostalgic scent
someone who was a child once
someone warm
someone who might be lovely
someone who she shares in-jokes with despite not knowing
personally.

The white girl on my arm could never know me like that;
never know *us* like that
that I take my shoes off at home

that I'm not actually embarrassed by my grandmother's accent
but mock her because it makes you laugh
that I don't call my grandmother 'grandmother'
that her hygiene is a point of bonding for me with any other person of colour
that I can't concentrate on her words when we're queuing for the plane
that I know the scent of danger in what she thinks is a friendly exchange.

   Pause.

When the white girl asks me, *'Wasn't it awkward… you know, cos…?*
I say,
'Hah, no, you know, I think any life lost is equally as awful as any other life lost.'

She giggles into me.

My words fester in the gap between my skull and the back of the brown girl's;
the space which can only have been the distance of leaning to kiss someone you love –

meaningless.
humiliating.

pathetic.

Words that turn their nose up and cram their eyes shut
words that ignore that they'd rather get off the bus
words that would rather take a slap to the face than face up to their pain

because at the end of the day what's the difference between a stop and search and her hands on me?

What's the difference between being stopped by the border guard and her asking this question before allowing me beneath her skirt?

    Pause.

The writer says that she raged that I stayed on the bus.

Raged that the thought of going home with the white girl,
to the white girl,
to a white embrace
to white thighs, white flesh, white skin, white words, white smirks
to white acceptance
was worth more than my dignity

worth more than our shared humanity

worth more than looking her in the eye even once

    Pause.

not even once.

    Pause.

When did you make yourself so ungrateful to your mother?

    Pause.

When did you make yourself so ungrateful to us who are the only ones who don't call you dangerous when the pressure gets too high?
Us, who are the only ones who don't see you as *threat* when you walk into a public space

Us, who are the first to make noise for you when they break down your door

who cradle you in our arms when you are broken and weeping
who do not tell on the weeping
who brush the tears from your cheeks
who do the weeping for you
who do the breaking with you
whose liberation is tied *to* you
who love you just as we love ourselves
if not more.

Us, who stand in the doorway ready to be trampled on when they come for your body.

Us, who no one blinks at when we are stamped into the doormat – and if they do blink –
in the moment of blinking can't really tell the brown girl from the doormat anyway.

    Pause.

It's 2009.

I'm another brown boy now.

Pause.

Pause.

I'd texted her the day before:

*'I need somewhere to stay, Oscar says I can't stay at his, I gotta go
Oceana with them though, it's the under-18s night.
I got new jeans for it'*

I was always too skinny for skinny jeans, but I got them cos it
was 2009 and skinny jeans is what everybody who wanted to
be taken seriously by white girls wore.
And yes, I wanted to be taken seriously by white girls, but to do
so I had to get to this under-18s night.

Oscar was the way in, the coolest white boy in the year, he
fit his skinny jeans perfectly. He wouldn't let me stay at his
though, *'just go home'* he'd said – as if that was an easy journey,
as if that was a self-evident conclusion.

So I asked the only person I knew who – I suppose in my year
9 brain I didn't know to put it like this – the only person who
loved me unconditionally and absurdly.

True, I exaggerated a bit.

I said I'd have to sleep on the street otherwise ████████████

██

██.

*'I need somewhere to stay, Oscar says I can't stay at his, I gotta go
Oceana with them though, it's the under 18s night.
I got new jeans for it.'*

jeans to pull girls in
jeans to pull white girls in
not her – unspoken
we don't pull girls like her – unspoken
girls with different coloured skins
ones who won't remind us who we are
ones who'd never let us stay over

██

██

████████████████

    Pause.

I never told her but the night was ████.
I should have got a belt for the jeans but a belt looked ████.
Oscar pulled two different girls, one was the one he said *I* was
supposed to pull, but she just kept asking whether Oscar had
ever mentioned her name.

    Pause.

Me and her fell out of touch a few years after that.

Seven years later I sent her this message:

*'hey, long time no speak
wht you saying*

u still about?'

Pause.

We met on the field – the field we'd all hung out in in Year 10. Her voice was different, not much else though.
She noticed my voice was different, too, though she didn't mention it.

She didn't mention much actually, listened a lot – as I say, not much had changed about her.
I told her I lived with a white girl for three years – we just ended things.
She seemed unphased.

I told her I needed to find myself again, I was going crazy – smoking hash and lying rent-free in a white girl's arms for three years really messes with your mind.
'I need to find myself again,' I said.

She didn't say, but is saying through this letter now:

You wanted to find yourself and came looking all the way in me? All the way in 2009?
You lost your brown boy self in whiteness and came looking for it back in me?
Ha. Isn't that always the way?

It reminds me of 2009 and the night you said you needed to somewhere to stay. Somewhere safe, somewhere that would always let you in, somewhere that couldn't turn you away. Somewhere to be a reprieve after the attempts to get white girls to desire you. Somewhere to come back to the parts of you that no matter how much you try to transcend, you cannot hide from when the sun has set.

It's 2016 and once again you need to find yourself somewhere safe, somewhere that will always let you in, somewhere that can't turn you away. Somewhere to be a reprieve after the attempts to get white girls to desire you. Somewhere to come back to the parts of you that no matter how much you try to transcend, you cannot hide from when the sun has set.

   Pause.

April 2019.

Her phone skips a beat.
A different brown boy's voice trickles into the kitchen

'it's me – you didn't – did you not save my number?'

   Pause.

'it'd be good to meet up'

   Pause.

She keeps the call short
I never find out that she cries as soon as she puts it down.
Crying for something, or from something, she can't tell
the tears just come.
Tears that haven't come for sixteen months.

Admittedly I have been AWOL, anything could have happened, true.
Last time we spoke was sixteen months ago when I was a daily Skype tone trickling into her room.
She would research family law for me – helping me get my divorce…

I know.

That's dedication.

White girls don't do that type of stupid ■■■ for brown boys.

I needed help though, to divorce my ex, and if there were any implications in the fact that she was the one helping me, they were just that: implicit.
I neither confirmed nor denied.

I just needed somewhere safe, somewhere that would always let me in, somewhere that couldn't turn me away. Somewhere to be a reprieve after the attempts to get white girls to desire me. Somewhere to come back to the parts of me that no matter how much I tried to transcend, I couldn't hide from when the sun had set.

After a couple of weeks I stopped calling though
went abroad to find myself

> *Pause.*

or maybe to lose myself by losing sight of her.

> *Pause.*

In 2019 I came back and called, said it'd be good to meet up again.
She said okay, obviously.
Hoping maybe I'd realised that no matter how much *I* want to be the protagonist of a white love story where she was just a footnote
we'd always be assumed to be waiting in the queue together
we'd always be in the interrogation room together
we'd always be chastised in the headlines together
always be spat at in the street together

when the legislation comes that *says go back where you came from*
I'll always be put back on the boat with her,
go back with her
go back to her
not with the white girls
not to whiteness
from whiteness
got to escape whiteness
with her.

So she says, *okay*.

   Pause.

We meet, and her voice is different, not much else though. She notices my voice is different too, though she doesn't mention it. She doesn't mention much actually, listens a lot – as I say, not much had changed about her.

I told her that upon reflection, I think she'd saved me – she'd helped me find myself – and now, a year later, I was here to thank her for that and to apologise that I couldn't have been to her what she was to me.

She didn't say, but is saying through this letter, now:

You found yourself in me and it took a year of absence for you to realise?

You lost your brown boy self in whiteness and despite me saving you, took a full year to notice?
In the meantime you didn't recognise that *I* might have disappeared?
Assumed I was a page that would always be left open.

Assumed I was a home that would always be waiting.
A pen never put down
a film on pause

██

███████████████████

It reminds me of 2017 and the night you said you needed to
get out of your head.
You were willing to cycle forty minutes through the rain
– which at the time seemed romantic but now seems ██████ –
just to find somewhere safe, somewhere that would always let
you in, somewhere that couldn't turn you away. Somewhere to
be a reprieve after the attempts to get white girls to desire you.
Somewhere to come back to the parts of you that no matter
how much you tried to transcend, you couldn't hide from when
the sun had set.

We sat, far apart – and do you remember how you cried?
I sat sheepishly both enthralled and afraid
that you'd allowed me to bear your pain
depended on me to do so
and I carried it with adoration and fear
fear that at any moment you might cry in someone else's living
room.

Because we raise brown boys to be conditional promises,
and we raise brown girls to want to be the white women brown
boys might make those promises to.

We raise brown boys to be exertions of domination,
and we raise brown girls to want to be the white women brown
boys might make those exertions over.

We raise brown girls to want to be white women
not to be them: impossible
but to want to be: a forever humiliation.

Humiliated every day by the reflection
humiliated every day by the skin tone
the hair
the facial hair – oh the facial hair
leg, arm, body – and I mean real body hair – not cute wispy leg
hair, not '*I'm a raging feminist*' armpit hair – I mean real body hair
arms that don't look right
legs that don't look right
bodies that don't look white
voices that don't do white
can't do right
can't white right

    Pause.

We raise brown boys to want the white girls we raise brown
girls to want to be
we don't want them to want each other, after all
but we want them to take each other, yes
be for each other, of course
secondary place prizes, disappointing.

We keep on at brown girls to keep trying to be the white
women we raised our boys to want our girls to be
they raise a child who sees his father wants his mother to be
another and she wishes she was too so he would want her.

They raise a child who wants to be white in a family that wishes
it was white
a family that's lost itself in trying so hard to lose itself.

And inevitably

when things go too far
when it's got too lost
will try to find itself again in the brown woman

will try to make home in the brown woman
try to be saved by the brown woman
who will be told she's too difficult
too complicated
too demanding
too brown.

A brown woman who will save them anyway.

Cos that's what brown women do
we save brown men despite being the skins they wish they
could shed
we save brown men despite being made into their footnotes
we save brown men despite never having been saved by them.

Us, who are the only ones who don't call you dangerous when
the pressure gets too high.
Us, who are the only ones who don't see you as *threat* when you
walk into a public space.
Us, who denounce you being maligned as paedophiles and
patriarchs.
Us, who are the first to make noise for you when they break
down your doors
who stand in the doorway ready to be trampled on when they
come for your bodies
who cradle you in our arms when you are broken and weeping
who do not tell on the weeping,
who brush the tears from your cheeks

who do the weeping for you,
who do the breaking with you,
whose liberation is tied *to* you
who love you just as we love ourselves
if not more.

> *Pause.*

But no one blinks when a brown girl is stamped into a doormat –

and if they do blink –
in that moment of blinking they can't really tell the brown girl
from the doormat anyway.

Suhaiymah Manzoor-Khan is an author, writer, spoken-word poet, speaker, and educator. She is the author of poetry collection *Postcolonial Banter* (Verve Poetry Press, 2019), co-author of the anthology *A FLY GIRL'S GUIDE TO UNIVERSITY: Being a woman of colour at Cambridge and other institutions of power and elitism* (Verve Poetry Press, 2019), and a contributor to *The Guardian*, *The Independent*, *Al-Jazeera* and *gal-dem*, among others.

NOTE: To perform this letter you'll need a suit jacket and shirt, some tomatoes, and a box that opens to reveal a selection of objects to dominate Simon with (for example: handcuffs, a gag, a dog collar and lead). In the original letter each section began on a new page; here, we've used an * to denote the beginning of a new page.

Dear Fake Simon,

Please read every word of this letter out loud.

Take your time.

Use a clear, projected voice.

Do not defer from the written text.

The text in *italics*, both read out loud – the audience needs to hear these words –

and also do – carry out these instructions as accurately as possible.

Do you promise to do these things?

I PROMISE.

*

You've entered into a legally binding verbal contract.
If you break this contract you will be held accountable.

·

Dear Audience,
You need to hold him accountable.
Do not allow him to break his promise.
Do not allow things to be half-done, mediocre, second-rate.
Call him out. Shout at him. Boo. Throw things. Can you do that?

Wait until they ALL answer.

·

Great, let's have a practice.

But first, in case the audience don't have anything to throw…hand out the tomatoes to your right.

·

Fake Simon, do this tongue twister.

Peter Piper picked a peck of pickled peppers.
A peck of pickled peppers Peter Piper picked.
If Peter Piper picked a peck of pickled peppers,
Where's the peck of pickled peppers Peter Piper picked?

Again but double time!

Peter Piper picked a peck of pickled peppers.
A peck of pickled peppers Peter Piper picked.
If Peter Piper picked a peck of pickled peppers,
Where's the peck of pickled peppers Peter Piper picked?

Again but backwards! Remember your vow Fake Simon, remember your vow audience!

Picked Piper Peter peppers pickled of peck the where's
Peppers pickled of peck a picked Piper Peter if
Picked Piper Peter peppers pickled of peck a
Peppers pickled of peck a picked Piper Peter

Take a fancy Shakespearian bow.

.

With some urgency, put on the shirt and suit jacket to your right.

.

Fake Simon is an actor, he'll be playing the role of Simon – a man who receives a letter.

Simon is a middle-aged, middle-class, white man in a suit. Just like Fake Simon.

> *Keep reading this line while you find Simon's voice. Keep reading this line while you find Simon's voice. Keep reading this line while you find Simon's voice. Time's up. Letter's here.*

Dear Simon,

Your handwriting is appalling – your surname is illegible, is it Clover or Clonen or Crones…? I can't make out your full name and I don't really remember your face. When the other receptionist asks me what you look like I say – white man, forties, probably slightly greying, probably slightly balding, bit chubby… has a head, shoulders, knees and toes. You all look the same.

> *Give us a twirl.*

So anyway Simon, you and your colleagues had a meeting with some other middle-aged white dudes at Walter & Conran a few months back. D'you remember? It was at three-thirty p.m. on the 2nd of September 2019, that's what your sign-in pass says. It was the same day that Farringdon Street was closed because someone was trying to jump off the bridge by Snow Hill, d'you remember me?

You come up to the seventh floor, out of the lift turn right, through a set of glass doors and you're at my reception. I think there were three other men with you.

You say:

HELLO MISS.

*

Once more with a big smile.

HELLO MISS.

*

Only kidding. You come to my reception and I'm the one who smiles and says 'Hello sir!'

You, you say nothing.

*

You don't return my smile.

*

You don't even look at me.

*

To begin with, I don't think anything of it. I don't know you, you don't know me, it's just some odd first encounter.
So I really look at you.
I'm willing you to communicate in any small way – a tiny half smile out of the corner of your mouth, a millisecond of eye contact, a nod, a grunt?

But no. Nothing.

> *Get up on your tiptoes, stay up on them until you're told you can stop.*
>
> *Continue reading the text.*

You start to fill in (really crappily as previously mentioned) the sign-in pass.
Your colleague thanks me and tells me who you're here to see.
I'm still looking straight at you.
You rip the sign-in pass out of the book. That's actually my job but… You rip it out and it tears in half and you say –

*

Nothing.

You leave the ripped pass on my desk and start talking to your colleagues. I pick it up, put it in a plastic lanyard and hand it back to you.

Your colleagues… Why don't they say anything to you? Or to me? Throw me a knowing glance, roll their eyes, something… anything that lets me know that they're not complicit and I'm not that insignificant. Or maybe they haven't noticed because I am that insignificant?

Our fingers are almost touching now, just a thin square of plastic between us…

I start thinking of a vending machine, feeling like a vending machine. Pop in your money, tap in B-6 and a Fanta just drops out. You don't say 'Hello' to a vending machine, don't smile at it, don't make eye contact – a vending machine has no eyes.

Your colleagues finish signing in and I say, 'do have a seat while I call Alastair or Charles or Gordon or Rupert or Other-Elderly-White-Guy-Name.'

You turn away and go and sit in the black leather chair by the white flatscreen TV.

> *Get off your tiptoes. Get on your knees.*

> *Continue reading the text.*

Dear Simon Scribbly-Surname, my name's Shireen Mula. I'm thirty-four years old. I live in Camberwell with my partner. I'm a playwright, I also lecture at London South Bank University and I temp on reception desks across the city. My mom's a nurse and my dad was a GP. They both came from quite poor backgrounds but worked really hard to get where they are. My father was a highly intelligent man but incredibly humble about it. I always remember when someone asked him what he did he'd say 'I work in a hospital.' He didn't want the status, the power, that comes with the title Doctor. He just wanted to be equal. I used to emulate that – I'd say 'I work in a theatre' and they'd assume box office or usher, maybe actor…but never playwright – the top of the hierarchy, the one who controls the actor's words and actions. I wanted to be just like my dad but then I realised he's a man and I'm a woman and those two things are not the same. A woman has to speak up about her successes, be dominant, assertive, to even begin to be seen as equal to a man.

Bark like a dog. Ten times please.

I've been a temp receptionist for thirteen years now and I've only ever worked with two male receptionists. Are the men all fast-tracked to higher-status, higher-paid positions? Is seeing a man in a subservient role a bit embarrassing for other men? Or do we just like to hear a woman's voice at the end of the telephone line while we imagine the rest of her?

I remember a businessman once saying to me 'so what do you do when you're not temping?' This time I say it, I say 'I'm a playwright' and he says, 'not going very well is it'.

Stand up Simon.

Take off your jacket. Let it drop to the floor.

Simon, I've got to say, I'm feeling pretty fucking angry.

Unbutton your shirt a bit.

What's that phrase again? Hell hath no fury like a woman scorned.

Bit more.

Power is a weird thing isn't it. You think you'll always have it and then all of a sudden the tables turn and someone new is in charge.

Bit more, don't be a prude.

When I tell the other receptionist about you she tells me the new manager, he keeps calling her 'blondie.' She doesn't like it. We swap stories. There's quite a few.

There's the one about the woman whose male boss used to tell her she looked anxious and rub her shoulders. She eventually had to take time off when her anxiety became too great.

It was a bit of a chicken and egg situation – which came first the anxiety or the shoulder rubs?

Then there's the one where two young businessmen at three p.m. every day, sit in reception just shooting the breeze about the bodies of the women they've just had meetings with.

Stories of women called 'girls' and men called 'sir'.

Simon. Let's do a bit of role play, shall we? Together, let's work this shit out.

'I'M SUPER HAPPY TO BE HERE WITH YOU SHIREEN – WORKSHOPPING, THROWING IDEAS AROUND, JUST HAVING A PLAY!'

You know all the right things to say. So, next time you walk into a reception what are you going to say when the receptionist says 'hello'?

'NOTHING.'

No Simon, bad Simon.

'ERM, I WILL PUNCH THEM?'

No.

'SPIT ON THEM?'

No.

'YELL AT THEM!'

Wrong again. Simon, what do you do when a man colleague of yours said 'hello'?

'WELL, I SAY HELLO BACK.'

Exactly.

'OOOOOOH.'

Give yourself a little pat on the head darling.

So, let's go again, you walk in and the receptionist says 'Hello' and you say:

'HELLO!'

Hello Sir, how can I help you?

'I'M HERE TO SEE MR WHITE-Y MCMAN-FACE.'

Sure, if you could please sign in for me and I'll give him a call.

'THANK YOU.'

End scene.

.

Wow! Sweetheart you did great!

'DID I REALLY DO OK?'

Absolutely! But maybe no more present tense dialogue, ok? It's not that you're bad at it exactly but...

Feel sad inside but make sure that no one sees it on the outside.

Are you ok?

You're not ok but make sure that no one sees it on the outside.

*

Dear Simon,

I brought your sign-in pass home and pinned it to my noticeboard to remember you by.
I'm writing because someone needs to hold you accountable.
I've brought you a gift which I think will help.
It's in the box to your right.

Open it.

*

Hold each item up, one by one, so we can all see.

In your head, decide which is your favourite.

*

Just imagine it.

*

Are you scared? What's it like to feel scared, Simon?

*

Hello sir!

...

Hello sir?

...

Who are you here to see?

...

Excuse me, did you hear me?

Hello sir!

...

Hello sir?

...

Who are you here to see?

...

Excuse me, did you hear me?

...

Sir... You're making me feel a bit invisible here...

...

It doesn't feel good.

Yeah, I could have said that and then maybe you'd have said:

'I'M SO SORRY, I WAS SOMEWHERE ELSE COM-
PLETELY. I'M TRYING TO REMEMBER EVERYTHING
FOR THIS MEETING, IT'S A REALLY BIG CONTRACT
AND I'M UNDER A LOT OF PRESSURE, AND THERE
WAS A MAN HALF ON HALF OFF THE SIDE OF THE
BRIDGE OUTSIDE AND IT SHOOK ME, A BIT.'

Yeah, I saw him when I was on lunch and it shook me a bit too
so I Googled and saw that suicide rates in men are super high.
Like eighty per cent of all suicides are men apparently.

'IS THAT RIGHT?'

Yes sir, and they say there's no work left to be done on gender equality.

'RIGHT. I REALLY DIDN'T MEAN TO MAKE YOU FEEL INVISIBLE.'

Thank you for explaining.

'COULD YOU TELL BARTHOLOMEW I'M HERE PLEASE?'

Of course, I'll give him a call.

Where you scared Simon? Is that what you were feeling? Were you scared about the meeting you were about to walk into? Were you scared after seeing that man on the bridge?

Boys will be boys.

We tell our boys that fear is weakness and tears are for girls so by the time they're grown, maybe they've completely lost touch with what it is to feel afraid or sad, let alone how to express those feelings.

Our boys will be the boys we make them.

I'm sorry I didn't say anything to you that day – give you the opportunity to explain, but I just couldn't.

The build-up of this feeling of inferiority or subservience women have, I have, inside my body from the years of small, small moments of being treated as though I'm nothing makes it really hard to speak up.

We are all the product of our society.

So Dear Audience, aren't we all a bit accountable?

Dear Fake Simon,

I patronised you, objectified you and told the audience to yell at you. You see, sometimes women... we think that doing horrible stuff to men balances out the horrible stuff that men have done to us. To gain equality, we think we've got to be more like men, but not just any man – the worst, most overpowering, aggressive type of man. But when I was choosing objects to place in that box to best assert my dominance over you, when I was imagining the effect of those items on your body, I realised that though your bodies are similar you're not really Simon. You both have a head, shoulders, knees and toes, a penis and a Y-chromosome but that's it. You're not him. So why am I punishing you?

I keep Simon's sign-in pass pinned to my noticeboard to remind me not to see all men as potential Simons.

Dearest Fake Simon, I almost put a dildo up you and I've no idea who you actually are!

What do you like to drink when you go out?

What kind of music are you into?

Are you watching any good boxsets at the moment?

What makes you laugh?

What makes you cry?

Who did you want to be when you were growing up?

Are you that person now?

What's your name?

No really, what is your name?

Please tell us your name.

*

It's been really wonderful to meet you.

Thank you and warmest regards,

Shireen

Shireen Mula is a playwright and theatre-maker. Plays include *The Rise & Fall* (Somerset House, 2017), *Soon Until Forever* (Theatre503, 2013), *Same Same* (fanSHEN & Ovalhouse, 2011) and *Nameless* (Arnolfini Theatre, 2010). She is a lecturer at London South Bank University.

IMAN QURESHI

NOTE: Where directions are in italics, please don't read them, do them. Everything else should be read out loud.

A request from Iman.

Can everyone with a British passport please stand at the back.

Everyone with a European, Canadian, Australian, New Zealand or US passport – stand in the middle.

Everyone with any other passport enjoy the rare occasion where you may stand at the front.

Please wait until the audience has moved before reading on.

This is an in-flight postcard from an anxious Pakistani passport-holder on a romantic holiday abroad

I, a white British passport holder, represent the recipient.

To my love,

I know you're excited about going on this romantic holiday together, but please forgive my clenched teeth and sweating palms – it really isn't personal.

I am excited, I promise, even though I look positively petrified.

In retrospect, it was probably a mistake to binge-watch multiple episodes of *Air Crash Investigations* the night before a long-haul flight.

The seatbelts feel too flimsy,
and are these elusive oxygen masks, that they assure us will just drop from above, even real?
Is there truly a life jacket under my seat,
and what good will it do when about seventy percent of our journey is over land, and not sea?
Surely it'd make more sense to store a parachute under there, or perhaps a giant bloody trampoline.
Why has no one thought of that before?

And where the fuck is the drinks trolley?

The least I can do is get absolutely trollied on mini Smirnoffs and Gordon's gins.

Because here's the thing that's been on my mind.

I should warn you – it's pretty macabre, so I hope it's okay that I've written it down on this cheery holiday postcard I picked up from the airport.

This thing is.

If this flight were to go down now, our bodies would be claimed by different countries.

Your beautiful body that I have loved with my own would be taken West, while my charred and embarrassingly unshaved limbs would be dragged East to a country I have never really known.

Don't look at me like that, I just didn't have time to shave. I promise I won't just let myself go now that we're – you know. I just ran out of time with packing and all.

Besides, I'll have a five o' clock shadow down my shins by the time we actually get to a pool anyway, so really I couldn't have planned it better.

Yes, yes I know you feel obliged to say, you don't mind hairy legs.

But I know that your standards of hairy are really talking about that light blond fluff that you have on your own white girl legs, and it can hardly be called hair.

Anyway. Where was I?

Right – when this plane crashes and we die,
you will be buried on British soil,
or cremated perhaps
– yes I think you'd prefer that –
scattered over the countryside where you grew up,
or into the South coast seas where you'd swim in the summers.

Or perhaps even just along the dusty disgusting South London street that we've lived these last five years,
your ashes blowing down alongside the grit and grime and dog shit that those fucking yob owners have again neglected to bag and bin.

Did you email the council about that, darling?
You said you would.
I'm not nagging.
Just reminding.

But yes,
if we crashed now,
and died on this here flight,
all our friends would attend your wake,
play the songs you loved,
Radiohead's 'True Love Waits'
or Nick Cave's 'Into My Arms'
— what a miserable yawn-fest of a funeral it would be.

But then they'd remember moments they shared with you.

The time you ate a whole raw lemon as a dare.

The time you got up in the face of a teenage kid who was trying
to mug you and, so astonished was he to see a petite white girl
transform into a terrifying hulk, that he gave up and ran away.

The parties you lit up,
The broken hearts you comforted,
The laughs you engendered,
The smiles you threw at strangers,
The seats you gave up for old ladies on the tube
— fragments of you in the form of stories that live beyond.

Perhaps the only missing piece would be me.

Me and my green passport would be lying limply in a morgue
in Pakistan,
so sadly,
I hope you'll accept my apologies
— I won't be at your funeral to tell all your guests how much I
loved you.

How I'd love running my hands through your hair, even though
you hated it and said it made it tangle.

Or how I loved tickling you till you cried and kicked me off.
Or how I had loved kissing your temples, at the exact point
your hair met your face, where that clean fresh smell of your
skin was the most delicious.

Because I'd be on the other side of the earth,
Being buried in a graveyard I've never seen,
In a city that was never home,
By strangers who share a share of the blood that once ran
through my arteries.

I'd be buried in an umrah shroud that was never my own
Because I have never been for umrah.
And prayers I hardly know would be recited over my grave in a
language I could no longer speak.

All this in a country where our marriage would never be recognized.
Our relationship never acknowledged.
Our love never known.

And as these anxious thoughts crash through my head, I look
at you, fast asleep beside me, snoring into your travel pillow,
which I am now regretting not buying too.

Two for twenty, a con, I'd said, smugly.
'Fine,' you'd replied, forking out the twelve for your own. 'Your
funeral.'

Ah the drinks cart – finally.
Yes I would like one. A vodka please.
What's that?
One to take the edge off or two to knock me out?

Make it three to quell the rising nausea which accompanies my
blind fear that this plane is about to career out of the skies,

hurtle earthwards, and smash across the Saharan desert in a way that is in actual fact a lot less romantic than the scene in *The English Patient* where Ralph Fiennes aka Voldemort gathers up Kristen Scott Thomas's limp body from a plane crash, carries her to a cave and makes love to her lifeless corpse.

That definitely happens by the way.
In the book anyway, if not the schmaltzy Hollywood film.
Because that's real love.
And trust me, the book is way better.

Okay so maybe just the two vodkas please, yes, sure, that's fine.

Knock back a couple of shots.

I'm fine.

I don't mind dying really.
That's the funny thing.
It's not the dying that scares me.
It's the dying abroad, that's a problem.

The passport thing, and a thing you will never really understand.

Being born in the place of your nationality,
of your parents' nationality,
and of their parents' nationality.

Having no attachment to anywhere other than where your little red book says you're from, having no immigration queues,
no scrutinizing looks,
no suspicious questions,
no unnecessary checks,
no random searches,
no seized baggage,

no restrictions on where you can live and for how long and how much you must earn,
no bits of archaic jingoistic versions of history you must learn to pass tests on what it means to be British.

No questions about whether you can bring your children
or what benefits you can claim
and what languages you must speak,
and how you'll benefit the economy,
and generally an expectation that you must be a citizen more upstanding than all the other citizens who are given their rights of citizenship by birth.

No wonder you're so fucking fast asleep, that even that screaming baby and bowel-clenching turbulence didn't wake you.

Your life is fucking blessed, really.

I know I sound angry,
and perhaps sometimes I am angry.
Sometimes I am angry that I have jumped through hoop after hoop to be with you,
but you can just be.
Sometimes I am angry that you don't understand.
Sometimes I am angry that you're angry on my behalf without knowing what it feels like, what it *actually* feels like to be discriminated against.

That's what it is.
It's legal discrimination,
legitimate discrimination,
proportionate discrimination.

Because at the end of the day,
The country in which we have both spent the majority of our lives
Views us differently.

The country that we both call home treats us differently.

And deep down,
deep deep down,
I can see you think that's okay.
That it's understandable.
That it's necessary.
And that really hurts.

I know this isn't the postcard you expected me to write you on
our honeymoon.
But here it is.

At the end of the day, my love,
as we set off on our honeymoon,
with wedding rings on our fingers,
our marriage certificate in case we need to prove our relationship
to get free champagne,
and our bikinis and sun screen
– Factor 50 for you, and a mere SPF 10 for me, because at least
I have melanin to my advantage –
this is what I really wanted to say:

You might think our love is free of borders
– that is your privilege,
to be able to claim identity in the borders within which you
live your life.

But in fact, our love is policed daily,
threatened daily,
by those borders that seem so invisible to you.

So as we fly at five hundred miles an hour across the borders
that have been carved onto this globe,
and I sweat
and panic
and inhale and exhale into the paper bag in the front pocket
of my seat
Know that it's not for fear of flying
Or even dying
But rather
For fear of being divided.

And as I watch you blink awake and fiddle with your in-flight
entertainment and adjust your seat back
I want you to know that though I love you across those borders
sometimes, it's difficult
when you don't see quite how hard they have been for me to
navigate.

And if we do go down,
and if it is the end,
I have one real wish
and I hope it's not too much to ask:

I hope souls in the afterlife are not policed as severely as bodies
in this world.

I hope the afterlife knows no borders, no immigration queues,
no customs stamps or luggage conveyor belts.

Because if that's the case then even if my corpse was taken East,
let me assure you that my soul would dig.

Dig through the earth,
right from the soils of Pakistan,

tunnel through Afghanistan and the Middle East,
swim up the Red Sea and into the Suez.

From there my soul would carry on,
across the Med,
further further,
right up the Bosphorus that divides Europe from Asia,
and burst onto the banks of your continent.

From there it wouldn't stop,
but carry,
carry on burrowing,
through Eastern Europe,
under and around the remnants of the Berlin Wall,
and onwards
before making the final stretch across the English Channel.

And my soul would do this, darling,
travel all that way,
evade all those borders in death as in life,
all to be with yours, my love,
all to be with you.

Happy honeymoon, my darling.

I cannot wait to spend the rest of my life with you. However
long – or short – that life may be.

With all my heart.
Your love

Iman Qureshi is an award-winning writer for stage, screen and radio. Her breakout play *The Funeral Director* (English Touring Theatre/Papatango, 2018) won the Papatango New Writing Prize and premiered at the Southwark Playhouse. Her short *Home Girl* was selected for the 2019 BFI Flare Festival.

*There is a bag on stage. Please wear what is inside. (It's a
pair of red trousers.)*

A note from the writer:

The writer would like to acknowledge that though she does
indeed have a baby and this is a letter to a baby, it should not
necessarily to be construed as being written to THE baby,
rather a baby.

Or as the back of a DVD case the writer has just found says
'any resemblance to actual persons, living or dead, or actual
events is purely coincidental.'

PS. Please don't take my baby.

He's my friend.

Dear Baby Boy,

You are one years old. This is not a letter of the unsaid. This is
said. I say this to you. You just don't say anything back. You can
be an asshole like that.

But as soon as you can answer I will stop saying this.

Because you can't know.

You can't know that I think I might not be the best. You can't know that sometimes you make me mad. And sometimes you annoy me. And sometimes I wish you weren't here.

You put your hands down the toilet. You chew on wires. You throw things out the bin. You turn the TV off while I'm watching. You throw food on the floor.

The food on the floor really pisses me off.

You cry when I don't let you smash my laptop on the ground. You broke my phone. You pull my hair. You gauge my eyes. You lost the TV remote for three days. I could only get onto Hayu on Amazon. I watched the whole of the *Real Housewives of Beverly Hills* again.

You made me do that.

I'm stupider now than I was before. And you are to blame.

I didn't want to be one of those white, middle-class mums you see smiling as they eat a garden salad and their kid screams and spits on them.

I wanted to be strict.

I wanted to be badass.

I wanted to be Lisa Vanderpump.

Or maybe Erika Giradi.

They're from the *Real Housewives*. Look what you've done to me.

I wanted a son with maximum respect.

I wanted to be a Ghanian mum.

I wanted to be Daniel's mum. Daniel's Ghanian mum. You did not fuck with that woman. I'd shout at my mum and Daniel'd be so confused. I want that.

But when I shout, you get cross.

When I stop you, you are confused.

If I cry, you think I'm laughing and you laugh. I wish that made me laugh. I bet good mums laugh. But I don't. I just cry more.

There is so much talk of being the perfect mum. Of how Instagram and Mumsnet has made us doubt ourselves and compete. How 'mums are superheroes.' But 'mums are only human.'

Fuck that, I thought.

Who are these sad women, comparing their parenting skills? I'm never going to do that. I actually have a life.

I'm just going to be…

quietly

fucking

amazing.

I'm not an honest person. I never have been. I wanted to be an actor as a child. Pretend to be someone else. Those bitches are amateurs. I went one further. I became a writer. I'm not just a liar. I cram my lies into other people's mouths. I marshal my differing opinions and confused thoughts and throw it out there so I don't have to confront a thing.

But then there is fucking Rachel.

With *My White Best Friend*.

Being honest. Being truthful. Here I am trying to give that a go.

Like I say baby boy, and you will learn this, honesty is not my strongest suit.

I'm shocked I'm not a better mum. I'm shocked I'm not a better person really. I always thought I was and I am just starting to learn that I'm not.

And that sucks.

But hey, baby, know why I had you. I lay in bed with the bright sunlight coming through my blinds on a hangover and thought 'enough of this now, y'know what a baby would stop me doing this shit'.

But here I am.

And here you are.

And I'm still doing this shit.

I'm going to tell you three things, but don't worry only one of them is true;

Number one. ████████████████████████

Number two. ████████████████████████████
████████████████████

Hang on, sorry. I just looked up bad mum confessions on the internet to get some inspiration. Someone 'admitted' they let the baby sleep in the car seat and another 'let their baby have pretzels for dinner'. Now I'm embarrassed.

Looking at you over there as I type,

with your cold breakfast pizza.

Gonna stop that confessional tract right there. Better get back to lying.

Is everyone is going to hate white people by the end of this? We were pretty bad by the end of Rachel's monologue. And now. Good God. Look at the state of the white person in this one. If my bad parenting incites a race war I will have peaked.

Now baby boy do not get me wrong. I love you very much. I have no regrets in having you. My regrets are all turned inwards. You are my mirror and I don't like what I see.

I've also given you a terrible haircut.

So I literally do not like what I see either.

I saw a therapist,

in this fictional universe where any resemblance to actual persons, living or dead, is purely coincidental,

and I told the therapist I would be happy whoever you turned out to be.

We were talking about my mum see and the terrible traumas inflicted upon me when she wouldn't let me wear trainers that flashed when you stamped.

And my God I wanted some trainers that flashed when you stamped.

And I told the therapist my mum had a lot of rules like that, she didn't want me to pretend to be someone I wasn't. Which the therapist countered with, 'but you were a child, how did you know who you *was* and *wasn't*?'

Were.

I silently corrected in my head.

'That was about her,' my fictional not-at-all-real therapist said, 'that was about who she wanted her kid to be.'

Oh the revelation that happened to me, baby boy! The Damascus road awakening of the terrible parenting that had been inflicted upon me, suddenly all my bad behaviour is validated! And of course I drop you when I'm drunk because I'm not a bad person just a very very traumatised trainer-less child.

How can a parent have so little sense of self that their child becomes their accessory? How weak and fragile an ego that extends the expectations they have for themselves onto their poor innocent child?

You know what I told that not-at-all-real therapist, baby boy? I told that therapist that you could be anything.

You can be a meth-addicted parking warden squatting on a houseboat with your gay lover Raoul. I don't care, baby boy! You be you! I am a cheerleader to your life. I love you no matter fucking what.

Because that's the deal of a parent isn't it?

Unconditional love.

And I get that and I'm signed up for that.

'What if' –

my-totally-fictional-therapist-who-in-no-way-seems-to-penetrate-my-well-constructed-woke-liberal-front

'What if' –

she asked

or he

either

they're not real

'What if he was…a county vet in red trousers?'

And suddenly, baby boy. Suddenly.

There I am.

I can hear the crunch of gravel under the tyres in the drizzling rain as we meander up the driveway to the detached pebble dashed three bedroom house in Surrey.

I can hear the two labradoodles,

they're hypoallergenic don't you know

barking already.

Francis and Zelda.

Named after the Scott Fitzgeralds even though I know you've only read *The Great Gatsby* briefly at school, are yappy and never have their nails – claws?

– what the fuck do you even call them on a dog –

cut and they jump up, leaving muddy pawprints across me.

You sigh and laugh as you run out after them, you look a little out of breath, sorry, you explain you were trying to force Zelda to eat her ham roll. It contains her medicine. The dog's diabetic.

Because of course it fucking is.

I look you over baby boy and say it's good to see you, yes you laugh and pat your stomach. Little too much maybe. I had noticed. I glance down at the slightly see-through white shirt straining at the top of *those* trousers that don't have a zip but only buttons. I don't know why they're made like that. And you call for your wife, call her away from 'the coal face'

which is what you call cooking.

On an Aga.

And I greet Jenny, as best I can.

'Mothers and their sons,' you say at dinner parties, about me and my daughter-in-law. 'No woman's ever good enough for their son.' And everyone nods and agrees because of course, that is why I don't like Jenny.

Of course,

that's the reason.

And out Jenny comes in her comfortable home crocs and toe nails that have not been cut and if they were would fly across the room like missiles because they're best described as chunky.

'Come on in folks!' she cries. 'I'm making gammon.'

.

.

.

.

Your father's here.

We make pleasant conversation.

I make a witty, if snide, remark about the kids who are either on their iPads or drawing on the actual table and he cuts me down about my constant need to judge others.

A quality I've always been rather fond of, but apparently is ugly… especially in old age. He says.

But we're all playing nice because it's our son's birthday, your birthday, and the kids have made him some lopsided mug and even the tennis coach sent a card.

The conversation turns to politics. I don't say anything. I try to talk to the children instead. I try to not hear what's being said. But I hear it all the same.

Your baby has cradle cap. Jenny says it doesn't need treatment, babies just grow out of it. I can see it from across the table. All the children have snot bubbling out their noses. You don't do anything. They're blonde and have gingham trousers on. You say how cute they are. Your babies make you very happy.

And you, *my* baby boy, sit proudly at the head of your table. You carve the incredibly fatty meat and spoon homegrown parsnips onto plates that were a real find in that flea market in Paris that you and Jenny went to ten years ago on your last 'kid free' holiday, and – and – and –

And as you can see, baby boy.

I am.

.

Fine.

.

With this.

I'd be fine.

If you were like that.

No...

no...

no judgement.

At all.

.

I seem to have finally separated my ego from myself, but now it's all over there, all sitting with you, and Lord knows I do not trust you with it.

My baby boy, out there, my mirror, that I can no longer control and I must not judge. Just out there reflecting me. This constant mirror satellite of myself, holding all my identity, but with none of my say-so. Just wandering round the world.

Being you.

Because parents should love their kids, and I know I'd love my kid no matter...

No matter...

What.

I'd love my kid no matter what.

I just really hope you're a meth-head gay boy.

Not...

> *The actor looks down to the trousers he was given. Back to the letter.*

And there's a real chance.

████████████

There's a real chance that you might be...

But you love your kid no matter what.

So...

Throw your food on the floor. Smash at the TV with wet hands. Chew up that pizza crust and try and feed it back to me.

My beautiful little man.

Because.

It seems.

It could.

It might.

Only get worse from here.

Anya Reiss is a writer for theatre and television. Plays include *Spur of the Moment* (Royal Court Theatre, 2010), *The Acid Test* (Royal Court Theatre, 2011) and *Forty-Five Minutes* (National Theatre Connections, 2013); her modern adaptations include *The Seagull* (Southwark Playhouse, 2012), *Spring Awakening* (Headlong, 2014) and *Oliver Twist* (Regent's Park Theatre, 2017).

We do these things for comfort. Tell the same story a lot. And I suppose it's important. Because now details of things slide through your grasp like grains of rice. Because now you've earned the right to only hear the ones you enjoy listening to. Where the beats are familiar. Where there are no twists or turns, or gaps in memory – only opportunities to add a better turn of phrase, a more flattering light. Because sooner than I'd like all we'll be left with are these agreed tellings, for Eid banquets which you won't cook. These words, to fill the chair where you won't sit.

And I tell the story a lot because in politics you need to have a pithy version of your genealogy ready to go. It helps, on the left, if Gramps once shook hands with Nye Bevan, or Nan personally chased the Queen Mother out of the East End during the Blitz. The reference points for us are different. You weren't a match girl. You weren't waiting for your soot-faced husband to come back from down pit. No one was a docker, a navvy, or hauled arse at dawn to work a factory line. I'm doing it again. Measuring you against the coordinates set by someone else's expectations.

It helps, in life, to rehearse a version of yourself. Pace in front of the mirror, practice placing your foot just so on the bottom step. Think about how you'll laugh later. The subtle augmentation of accent to suit your audience; learn the codes, and switch between them. The key to performing is to look like you're not. You laugh at some of the tellings like you're a stranger to yourself. I take that as permission. I tell your story often, as though I'll feel more myself for it. I don't have a story of how I got here, so I borrow yours instead.

Caledonian Road, 1954. You pop up outside the tube station like the first pin dropped on the map, the map of all of us. You're seventeen and you're not dressed properly for the weather. The clothes you brought with you are too thin. Your face is too trusting. You leave a mother, a sister, a dead father in Kolkata. You leave your school friends and full-time education there too: you don't find it again until decades later, in Nottingham, when you've got three grown-up children and an acrimonious separation under your belt.

London's a cold city. You work, or you freeze. Your landlady's tight with the central heating. The narrow window for hot water doesn't line up with your shift at the hospital, so you scrub your skin raw under the cold tap to get the sweet stench of human frailty off you when you get home. You eventually buy some thick knits, but that's no armour against the teddy boys on the corner by North Road. White lads, with their switchblade glances. It's not so much that they shove you to the ground, more that the pavement has become an extension of the air. One minute you're walking through it; the next it knocks the breath out your cheek and the taste of iron fills your mouth. On the good days, it's just spit and 'Paki' and 'Wog' rolling off your retreating back.

You told me never to respond to anything which isn't my name. You told me to wear it like my mother gave it to me. Which is strange, because nobody calls you by yours. There's the one printed in your passport, and its various iterations mangled by the melanin-deficient. There's the nickname from your baby sister, which neither of you grew out of. And there's Mamoni. Precious mother. It was just my mum, my uncle and my auntie who are meant to call you that. But somehow the usual Bangla honorifics never fit, and other people's Nans are the kind of old biddies who don't season vegetables and vote UKIP.

So Mamoni outgrew the usual generational boundaries. It escaped the clutches of the beanpole family. Your friends call you Mamoni. My friends call you Mamoni. Somehow your name exceeds your blood, your legal ties, your many homes and jobs. It's used on three continents. I heard it in every accent under the sun. Somehow Mamoni gets to be a mother like no man can be a father. You're at the centre of every network I know. The first pin, as the map sprawls around you.

I'm often on Caledonian Road. My best friend lives there, the one you think is handsome and no good. I find myself walking the same route as yours from the tube station to his gaff, or out on the booze run. And our parallel lives, the ones separated by sixty years and a generation in between, could not be more different. I'm always happy even on my worst day. Never alone. Hanging out with a friend who grew up in the same neighbourhood in North London, went to the same school. We drink like sailors and bicker like siblings and no one up in this dunya understands me better. Best friends. Diaspora kids. Same slang, different football teams.

I say I'm Bengali. My passport says United Kingdom. But I've more North London in me than anything. My mother was born in Wood Green. I've got PG inked on my ribs. Our neighbourhoods, like our bloodlines, like our matriarchs, contain the uncontainable. I've never left that flat without laughing at jokes told in three languages. Without carrying all that warmth with me when I head outside. And in another time I might pass you by at seventeen years old walking the other way. Shivering. Carrying us on your young, slim shoulders.

There's rougher versions. Ones where you speak unkindly, and I make another bad decision. I put another foot wrong. You talk bitterly of regrets. Of grudges left unavenged. But if I had to tell this story honestly, I wouldn't have told it at all. Some things should be left where you first heard them, corroding a hole through the kitchen table. You have a right to be forgotten too. I collide with you on Cally Road, and choose to remember the determined soul in a flimsy sari. It's a kindness, I think, to let the worst recede out of view.

Ash Sarkar is a journalist and political activist. She is a Senior Editor at Novara Media and a contributor to *The Guardian* and *The Independent*.

SOMALIA SEATON

NOTE: This letter must be read by a Black womxn, wearing a party hat.

Right, first off…

First off it says…

It says you lot have to sing 'Happy Birthday' to me

It does!

Technically it's not even my birthday yet – technically it's at midnight – and I'm gonna be fifteen – and Jesus gets an eve and a day – so I don't see the problem to be honest

I'm not lying you know, it's what they've asked for…says it here in black and white

I'll show it to you – I will – if you don't believe me

Says whoever's around when you open this letter, must sing you 'Happy Birthday' – with enthusiasm – not any old dry crusty – out-of-tune something, neither – and they must sing black version – not the white one – it's what it says – don't blame me –

Sings.

'Happy Birthday To Ya' – That one

'You know it?

'And the moment they finish singing' – that's you lot – 'You're allowed to carry on reading.'

Right then.

Is that okay?

Cool.

Go on then

I'll count you in

You ready?

Five, four, three, two, one

Once the audience have finished singing, continue reading.

Say thank you

That was for me, thank you!

So I'll begin

Dear Lia,

Happy birthday.

You'll soon stop calling yourself that. Somalia is a beautiful name, don't let the legacy of The Somali Woolwich yutes – and their rampage through Catford – make you whisper your name when engaging with people, only a dickhead would assume that you had Woolwich yute affiliation because your name is Somalia. Any confusion over where you pledge your allegiance will be rectified when you start hanging around the estates near ███████ with ████████ – pretending you're about that life – knowing you are most certainly not about that life – don't roll your eyes – yes, you know people – but no – you ain't bad – remember I told you – though you will meet your first love there – yes – eventually you'll stop snogging your friends in toilet cubicles and sleepovers – a real boy will stick his tongue down your throat – he'll stick a few other things inside of you too and you'll fucking love it. But for now focus on snogging girls.

Besides, your parents wanted to name you after an African country and this is the one they chose, so don't let any foolishness get in the way of the beauty in that

Yes, ████ used to sing 'S-s-somalia-s-s-s-somalia YOU NEED FOOD' in primary school – yes she was a stupid cow – and yes laughing about famine involves a special kind of stupid – plus *Red Nose Day* and *Comic Relief* parading the poverty-stricken versions of Africa around without any historical context as to how parts of the continent ended up like that will enhance her ignorance of her own ancestry – but for some context – that girl was also the eldest of five kids, her mum spent most of their money on crack and she never knew her dad. And well, both your parents would always come to parents' evening – so she assumed you had it all. I won't say no more, because you'll buck up with her again, and I'll let her explain it all herself. But she'll trigger your deep sense of compassion and empathy – and it's great – but I need you to keep an eye on that trait of yours.

Anyway, I digress – I do that –

Happy birthday, you beautiful Queen.

I love the navy kappa jacket you just conned your dad into buying you at The Glades.

You're clearly about to rinse it off at school, so I won't waste my breath, though do try and keep it safe if you can – I mean – you won't but I wish you would, because they're all the rage with the hipsters, these days – the 'Daddy bought me a pony and a rooftop flat in Kensington' type chicks – the ones that choose to 'slum' it in Pecknarm instead – the ones with the dusty Reebok classics and stiff upper lips – think ███████ – she'll be one of them in a couple decades, what a mess – don't invite that bitch to your party neither. Yes, asking you if you use your hairbrush to brush your pubes – knowing full well that hair came from your head – is a fucking parr. It wasn't an innocent question neither – it was dehumanising and someone should have told her to shut the fuck up.

And yes, calling another female a bitch – a fourteen-year-old one at that – might be problematic, but not everything that you do needs to be perfect – sometimes call a horrible bitch, a horrible bitch. In any case she's not your friend, you'll soon see.

So look, it's been a full-on year, for you.

And not just because you got caught teefing Moschino notepads and stuffed animals from Paperchase and Clintons – I know you're still sporting that long PVC coat from Mum's shop – but she didn't give it to you so you could stuff stolen shit into the lining of it – don't do that again.

You also moved house – to a new area – you went away with the family – I know you loved it – I want you to know the things that you found weird on that trip, really were – you didn't imagine it and it's okay that your memory feels foggy for now – I understand why you slump – but your body is yours and older men looking at fourteen-year-old girls are the ones that should slump not you – I know this will take time – but I can't wait to see you fully in your height.

And you're gonna keep forgetting things – don't screw up your face – you will – not all of that will be intentional – you'll dissociate from most of it – because...

I'm skipping ahead here – it's just – there's a lot that I want to acknowledge

So

Reading this is gonna be difficult – reading this aloud in front of whomever you have fast up yourself and invited – is also going to be difficult – but you are held – even when you can't see the arms wrapped around you.

You are held.

When you were woken from your sleep to sounds of her screaming and his eyes dead like night and his flesh beating repeatedly into her skull – you did the right thing. They'll tell you that sometimes men hurt women, and despite it being wrong, it doesn't mean that they don't love them, but it does – certainly not in the right way – not in a healthy way.

You don't hurt what you love. That is not love. You'll really understand that in five years or so, when you very nearly repeat the aforementioned pattern – but that is not your portion and we're not gonna get into all of that, right now.

You'll learn also that when men hurt women, we sometimes cover up for them, to protect them ahead of protecting ourselves – that women of your own hue will feel strongly about protecting the men of our hue – above all else – because the world treats them like dangerous prey – and you'll internalise all of this and regurgitate it when protecting the men in your life ahead of yourself – like it's cool, but it is not. Yes, Babylon is fuckeries. But it's okay to put yourself before the black men in your life, you need protecting too.

I need you to know, that night was not okay – what you witnessed was not okay – and it will stay with you, it will teach you obedience.

But when Mr ▇▇ raises his voice to you in your maths class, because you can't find your protractor – and you reply with, 'What am I gonna do with a pie chart when doing my food shop at Sainsbury's, Sir' – first of all you, my dear, will not be shopping at Sainsbury's – you'll be shopping at Aldi – don't screw up your face – and second of all Mr ▇▇ was a dick for sending you out of class and giving you a Saturday detention – it was an important question.

Mr ▇▇, like many men like him, isn't ready to be challenged by a girl like you just yet. I know your dad has already told you this in his own way – and I wasn't particularly here for it at the time – but look – you can't get away with stuff like a Sarah or a Ruby – your skin is black and your limbs are long.

You stand out. People notice you. The rules are a little different for you.

When Mr ████████ calls your parents into school and tells them they're going to suspend you because you are still refusing to talk to ████ – he was out of line for that – and when he told your parents that you have stopped the whole year group from talking to her too – nope, you were never responsible for all of that mess – and when he summarised with, 'Somalia is too influential, she operates as a ring leader, and it's uncomfortable for many of her year group' – yes, he was displaying his prejudice towards you – both at your parents daring to send you to that school and at you being a tall black teenage girl that dwarfed the many short white vulnerable females you hung around with. God forbid that you too might be vulnerable.

This will stay with you too. But here, you did not display obedience. Hold on to that. Furthermore, you better just sit in the glory of you being influential. Don't let anyone tell you that you can't or should not lead.

When ████████ started punching you in English class and Mr ████████ ignored it all until you finally hit him back and you ended up on the floor with a boy on top of you pounding away at you – again Mr ████████ will call *you* – a female – a trouble-maker – an instigator – he will share pictures of red marks on the white skin of ████████ – a boy – and your mother will remind Mr ████████ you are a girl – *and* black – the bruising *is* there. You will come to know that, like your bruising, your vulnerability will go unnoticed – Black before Female – that's what they see.

They'll be many more boys that try to fight you in school – in fact you will never ever have a physical altercation with a woman – I'm sorry to say it – but there'll be many more ████████ that raise their hands to you in educational settings – and I'm sorry about that – you're taller than most of them – and black *and* a girl – this stirs something primal in them – something violent. The world teaches boys and men to conquer women – so that's what they'll aim to do – don't let it shrink you.

Sidebar – a fucking weirdo will approach you in Oxford Circus in about fifteen years, he will beg you to follow him to a hotel and beat him senseless – this information is too much for you at your age – but beware of the subtle and not too subtle ways you are objectified and fetishised as a woman, a black woman, a tall black woman.

Anyway, Mr ████ is a racist, Somalia.

You're going to meet many more of them. They'll adorn titles such as teacher, manager, friend's dad, friend's brothers, friend's grandfathers, directors, playwrights, artistic directors. What they'll all share in common is that LIBERAL badge of honour they've all got tattooed on their forehead – but they're the worst ones. We'll come back to this.

A quote-unquote prolific white male playwright leading an international residency for writers, will ask the group to share a piece of art, an article and music depicting where you've all come from. When you share the original blog post that led to Reni Eddo-Lodge's award-winning book *Why I Am No Longer Talking To White People About Race*, he, the only other Brit in the room, will seek to illegitimise your connection to Reni's work. Instead of the interest and intrigue that he affords your white peers, he will interrogate you, the only non-white person in the room, on whether you consider yourself British and whether you believe England to be a racist country. He will sit back in his chair, cross his legs and stay silent for the rest of your talk. He will form an old boys' club with the male writers in the room and he will bring sexual innuendos into every interaction he has with the female writers. He will shower you with a strange cocktail of disdain and wondering eye. Inserting sexual content into pleasantries whilst simultaneously making you feel invisible and stupid – that's what he attempted. He will make other women in that room cry. He will disorient you, with a constant onslaught of abuse of power and gaslighting.

Men like him are very clever about which version of themselves they present to each group they encounter. I want you to be aware of him in advance – because there's so much about this industry you'll eventually find yourself in that'll make you think you've imagined things. You won't have imagined anything.

You won't recognise it at first, but this encounter will cause you trauma – and you will remain silent – that is okay – but when you remember how to speak – do speak about it.

Moving on.

So I'm just gonna say it.

You are in love with Ruby. Don't freak out, I'm just calling it as I see it. It's cute – it is! You're allowed to be in love with your best friend. You're allowed to fantasise over her, and if you both want to find yourself locked in the toilet cubicle again, honey, that's absolutely fine.

But stop letting ███████ call you his little sister, when all he is interested in is using you as his entry point to your white and mixed-race friends. ███████'s mum would box him upside his head if she knew he was going down on Ruby in the basement cloakroom – and he knows it.

When Mrs ▮▮▮▮ receives a phone call from an anonymous concerned parent that an underage Ruby and an older but still underage ▮▮▮▮ have been having sex, she'll call the police to the school instead of calling their parents first – you'll be reminded of the correlation between blackness and danger once again, and so too will he.

When Ruby's brother starts asking her why she keeps bringing that 'black guy' round to the house – asking her why she can't date a white boy – you'll sit in the kitchen looking at her giant fish, pretending you can't hear them.

You'll do the same every time Ruby's lovely mother drives her really long fingers into your afro and makes random excitable noises.

And again when well-meaning people of the same hue congratulate you on how well you speak, whilst people of *your* own hue comment on how white you sound.

I'm gonna say this to you once, baby girl, we too are capable of internalising this shit – intellect is not synonymous with whiteness. Close your ears to the subtle ways in which they feed you this.

So

All your friends have been having sex for a while, and apart from the leg of your giant teddy bear Sam, the only thing you've been rubbing your vagina on is your toothbrush – and the shower head – I know it was Ruby's idea – but Ruby used to stick money in her knickers and claim that she would orgasm like that – you can't listen to everything Ruby says, babes.

I know you want a boyfriend, and I know you want a period too.

I know your mum still hasn't spoken about your trip to the hospital and all the things the doctors have said you'll have to do. And I'm sorry.

But doctors aren't God. I know, I know – you fucking hate it when Mum says that – but look.

I can't say too much, but believe me when I say there is power between your thighs – your body is working for you in ways that not even those doctors of yours can contain.

It's okay that you are switching off – not taking it all in – it's too much for your teenage, not-yet-fully-developed brain.

I want you to know that I fully acknowledge that you are not being supported. That you are pretending to be on the same pill as your friends, that your periods are rare and your breasts are yet to grow. That you struggle to concentrate – how the fuck could you concentrate – and no extra consideration can be given for your exams – because nobody speaks – not even you – why would you – it's not the thing we do – Mum's told you – and Dad too – we don't take inside business outta door – but that's how disease festers – it goes unseen in dark pockets of the womb – rotting away at what was once vibrant and living cells.

I can't begin to tell you how sorry I am that no one was there to hold you – to tell you it would be okay.

But those parents of yours – your mum and dad – they became parents at twenty-five and twenty-eight – do you have any idea how fucking young that is? They're still learning – they're not gonna get it right all the time – you'll learn to give them space to be human – they Love You Deeply.

When ▮ came back to school and started hurting herself – and ▮ soon followed suit – you found the perfect set of people to help you conceal your pain – in their problems you could find a little bed to sleep upon – you'd lay your sorrow to sleep – whilst you and your teenage brain, with its lack of ability to contain, rolled around in the playground of your friends' pain. What happened to both ▮ and Marni is awful – I know you keep getting taught that men are dangerous – yes they are – but you'll find the ones that ain't.

▮ and ▮ need you and you need them to need you, too – remember we spoke about co-dependency – that's what this is – they help you escape from yourself – you help them to heal, too. It's not your fault – that shit was passed down to you – be patient – we've got this – promise you – for real.

I'm sorry that was the case. That no one caught on to what was happening with you.

I'm sorry that all of those most closest to you have learned to call you the reliable one – the one that is always there – leaving you unseen – I'm sorry that you've been caught in this strange place of feeling like you needed to be smaller, more palatable, less intimidating, take up less space so that you could feel safe. Whilst desperately needing someone, anyone to look – to really look beneath your Might and see you are vulnerable and also in pain.

I say all of this because I know, no one ever has. I want you to know that I see you – I'll hold you – I'll continue to have your back.

But

I need you to do something for me

Okay?

And you're gonna need to trust me

You are Me

And I am You

And I'm so thankful for you getting me to this spot

But you're not a commodity for people to consume

You were not born to be obedient to demands of others

You and I can't exist like this no more

When you let go of those buds you and I can continue to bloom

I need you to let me begin

I'm doing the work to process all that you were forced to consume

But please let go and let me bloom

Something is growing in me and I can't nurture it if you keep running scared

We are safe now, baby girl.

Trust me.

You and Me.

Me and You.

I write you this letter as you end your second cycle two sets of seven and many more await you

As I approach my fifth. I need you to walk alongside me – stop consuming me with the scars of yesteryear – and let me live.

I'll say it again

And I'll remind you if ever you feel fear

We are safe now.

We are safe now.

We are safe now.

Somalia Seaton is a playwright and screenwriter. Her plays include *Red* (Tonic Theatre, 2017), *Fall of the Kingdom, Rise of the Footsoldier* (Royal Shakespeare Company, 2017; finalist for the Susan Smith Blackburn Prize), *House* (Clean Break, 2016), *Crowning Glory* (Stratford East, 2014, shortlisted for the Alfred Fagon Award), *Curly Fries and Bass* (Lyric Hammersmith), *Mama's Little Angel* (The Yard, London), and *Hush Little Baby* (Open Works Theatre Co./Soho Theatre).

NINA SEGAL

NOTE: Text written in italics should not be read out loud.

On the stage is a cool box, a lamp and a letter. The performer opens the cool box and removes a large block of ice. They place the ice below the lamp, then open the letter and read it out loud. Over the course of the performance, the heat of the lamp causes the ice block to begin to melt.

This isn't easy for me to write.

I've tried a few times – tried different approaches, different angles. Different versions of me, of you. Of us. Because even after all this time, even with all this distance between us, we are still, aren't we, an 'us'. Aren't we?

But still – it isn't easy.

What am I worried about? So many things. So many, many, many things. But, specifically – I suppose I'm worried that you'll find me angry. And stop listening. Or that you'll find me boring. And stop listening. Or that you'll say you've heard it all before, that it's not news, it happens all the time. And stop listening.

And that's true. It does happen all the time – is happening all the time. To more people than you could possibly imagine. But still – isn't that more reason to talk about it, not less?

So. Here goes.

The first thing I want to say is: I forgive you.

That's not easy for me to say, or to believe. But it's true. I forgive you. I can't say that I understand completely, I can't pretend that I'm not angry, I can't hide all the sleepless nights, all the impossible mornings, the sun barely visible through the thick dark. I can't say that I don't wish – every day – that it had been different. But I can say I forgive you. What else is there? What other option? It's done now. You did it, a long time ago now, and it's done. And so there's nothing else that can be done. Not now.

I thought I heard a bird call this morning. It made me think of you – nature always does. I opened the window a crack, searching for the bird – even though I knew that it was only my imagination.

A memory of you, or some strange version of memory.

I try, but still – I can't pretend that I'm not jealous. Of you. Your life. I look at photos – I admit it, yes, I do – I look at photos of your life. Holidays abroad, long weekend drives, new clothes and bags stuffed full of shopping. Complicated meals made with brightly coloured vegetables, with snow on the ground outside. I look at photos of your perfect life with all your piles of perfect stuff – and I want it. All of it. I know I shouldn't, but I do. I want it.

I saw a photo of your family. Your children. Two children, isn't it? Or three? And all of you happy. Carefree. Unaware and oblivious – not thinking, of me or anyone else. Of the effect – the harm – you cause. That you cause, even in your happiness, by just existing. And why should you?

I put away the photograph. I don't like to feel this way – I try hard not to feel this way. But I look around me and it's just – grey. Dust clouds. Smog. I don't mean to sound dramatic when I say this, but I have nothing. Not compared to you.

I wish that I could open the window.

I'm sorry. I don't mean to sound accusatory. And what good would it do anyway, to accuse? You played the innocent, right up until the end. The guiltless party – the victim, even. None of what happened was your fault. None of it was your responsibility. You turned away from the pain you caused and focused on yourself – your needs, your pain. And I don't blame you. It's a human instinct, isn't it, to look away from pain? From the things that you can't fix.

The things you don't believe that you could fix.

It's not that you weren't aware things were broken. You knew. It was obvious. But it scared you, so you turned away. Retreated. Held up your hands – offered apologies, excuses. But no suggestions. No solutions. Did you?

The things you used to say. Like mottos, mantras, repeated so often there ceased to be another possibility:

'I don't understand.'

'I don't have time.'

'I can't imagine how to fix this.'

Was it a failure of imagination? Of understanding? Not time, surely. That's the only part I find hard to forgive. There was time. We had time. Twelve years – it's not nothing. But I think, really, whatever it was – twelve years, twenty, thirty – it wouldn't have been enough. Not to make the change you needed to make.

The change I needed you to make.

I didn't ask for much, did I? I didn't ask the impossible. Really, even small things might have been enough. Slight adjustments. Daily changes. Thoughtfulness, really, was what was needed, wasn't it? Thoughtfulness and a bit of effort. An awareness of actions – of consequences. A bit of thought, for others.

Is that a small thing? Or one of the biggest?

Maybe it wasn't about the small things. Maybe it was too late for that, by then. Maybe what I wanted – needed – was a grand gesture. A clear sign. Maybe I needed you to stand up and go out into the street, with a speaker or a megaphone or just your own voice and shout, shout loudly, until everybody noticed, and everybody knew how much you cared. Maybe I wanted you to write it in six-foot letters on a public wall, or on a banner hung from the balcony of a government building. Maybe I needed you to scale walls, climb fences, lie down in the road and refuse to move – until everybody knew how much it mattered. How much you cared – about me, about us. The future. Our future.

But you never did that, did you? Did you stand in the street and shout? Chain yourself to railings? Lay down on the road, the runway? Did you raise your voice, at all? Maybe you did. But it wasn't loud enough for me to hear.

The last thing you said was that you didn't understand. You didn't see it coming, never imagined it would be this way. End this way. To the bitter end, you didn't understand. As the waters rose around your ankles, you stood there, numb and disbelieving. An ice shelf crumbled into the sea as you said, 'Hold on, tell me again?' The noise of the hurricane drowned out your question, I couldn't hear you over the roar of the incoming wave. 'I can't believe this is happening,' you said, again, as the screen in your hand burned bright with forest fires, once again. 'I didn't see the signs,' you said. You took off your shirt. It was November. Outdoors. You walked inside, where it was air-conditioned.

Did you know what you were doing? Maybe not. I never had the chance to tell you, not directly, not before.

So. Here goes:

You tore my world apart. This is not a metaphor. Fractured it, broke it to pieces. This is not a metaphor. Scorched the earth, blighted the land, poisoned the rivers, burned it all to the ground, left it charred and useless. You set our house on fire and left me with nothing but the crap, the mounds of crap you left behind. None of this is a metaphor. You did this. You really did.

You might be gone, but I look out my window at the eternal remains of you. A plastic shampoo bottle. A plastic bag. A great mound of earth, raked over, but barely covering the memories. You have become immortal, unwittingly. You left, decades, centuries ago, but here you are. And here is your effect, on me and everyone, forever.

I can't send this letter because I don't exist yet. I don't know yet about any of this. All the things that you will do; have done. And all the things you won't. I don't know about any of that and by the time I do, you will be gone. And any chance with you.

But – I forgive you. And I understand. You were busy. You were tired. You had things on your mind. You put yourself, your needs, your immediate concerns, first. And that's normal, isn't it? To put yourself first? That's a survival instinct. You put your survival first. I wasn't a priority, even if you wanted me to be. Even if you knew, deep down, I should be.

I'm not angry. I do have one question, though. Could things have worked out differently?

I suppose that was up to you.

> *Behind the performer, the following four slides of text are shown.*

SLIDE ONE

The world's leading climate scientists have warned that we have twelve years left to make the changes necessary to limit global warming to a maximum rise of 1.5 °C.

SLIDE TWO

Any warming above this will significantly increase the risk of drought, floods, extreme heat and poverty for hundreds of millions of people, now and in the future.

SLIDE THREE

To avoid exceeding this level of warming will require 'rapid, far-reaching and unprecedented changes in all aspects of society'. (The Intergovernmental Panel on Climate Change, 2019)

SLIDE FOUR

I don't want your hope.
I don't want you to be hopeful.
I want you to panic.
I want you to feel the fear I feel every day.
And then I want you to act.
I want you to act as you would in a crisis.
I want you to act as if our house is on fire.
Because it is.
– Greta Thunberg, 2019

The ice continues to melt.

Nina Segal is a playwright and screenwriter. Her plays include *Assembly* (Donmar Warehouse), *Dismantle This Room* (Bush Theatre/Royal Court Theatre), *Danger Signals* (New Ohio), *Big Guns* (Yard Theatre) and *In The Night Time (Before The Sun Rises)* (Gate Theatre/Teatro Belli/Atlantic Theater Company's Amplified Series/Orange Tree Theatre).

I am not Tolani's ex!

But I represent her ex and all the other men she has fancied, loved and imagined unrealistic romantic situations with. Men that she has ended up hating because we – sorry, *they* – let her down.

So although I am *a* man, I am not the one who did *this*. So to make it clear, this is *me*, being *Tolani's ex*, written by *Tolani*.

Here it goes.

Tolani was always going to write stories about me. I mean it's *me*.

I am, or should I say *was*, the main protagonist of her life, for most of her life. So, of course, she was going to tell stories about me.

But the stories aren't really what I thought they would be.

They don't flow. They're not melodic nor rhythmic.

The good has been smudged with the bad. And I know that it wasn't *all* good *all of the time*, but I expected poetry.

You know…

'Roses are red, violets are blue, I lost true love, the day I lost you.'

That kind of shit.

And she tried, she really did, But I guess I sucked that out of her. I guess she couldn't find a poetic way to say, 'I hope the love of your life cheats on you with a below average rapper.'

I mean I get it, our story didn't go according to the dreams I sold. You see, I made her believe our story would be something out of a rom-com. I made promises without actually committing to anything. I did everything the men before me taught me.

I would hold her chin, lift her face up, look her dead in the eye and say some slick shit like, 'I see you in my future' with no vision of what this future would be.

I promised to make her feel like that Shania Twain song she loved. You know the one. It goes...

> *Sing.*

'Looks like we made it look how far we've come, my baby.'

She would listen to that song over and over again, and every time it played she had this hopeful smile on her face. A smile that pleaded with me to make good on my promises. So I knew I had to play the song *that* night.

It was the only thing that would have made things better, it would have made her hopeful again.

And it did. For the three minutes and fourteen seconds that song played for, we were good.

That's a lie, we weren't *good*. But I like to remember it like we were. You see that's the thing about nostalgia. It's kinda mad still. It has a way of over-romanticising situations. It taints memories and leaves you with the parts that *felt* good.

It means I remember that time Tolani wore that red dress that made her body look MAAAD.

But it fades out the part where she slid down my bedroom door in tears, using the same red material to comfort herself because she found texts on my phone.

It also means that instead of focusing on how I dragged her out of a party, I sit on the memory of the drive home, where I was the *man!* The man whose girlfriend did *not* go out raving. Because why would my wifey be in a club, clubs are for skets.

I remember the smile on her face when I said that, she must have found it romantic.

And of course, it's nostalgia that means I only dwell on the memory of my hands placed on her waist and hers draped over my shoulders as we swayed side to side to Shania singing,

Sing.

'We mighta took the long way, we knew we'd get there someday. They said I bet they'll never make it. But just look at us holding on. Still together still going strong.'

I needed her to believe those lyrics *that* night, more than any other time before, I needed her to *buy* the dreams I was selling. That was the only way I could make things okay, the only way I could make up for letting her go alone.

But she had to go alone, what good was I going to be sat with her?

Plus I had a football match that day and football meant a lot to me. And I'm not even trying to gas it, but if I *didn't* get injured, I *would have* gone pro.

.

I mean we did have other options. The nurse told Tolani that she could have had it adopted, but when Tolani asked her how to hide the bump from her mum for nine months, she wasn't much help.

Then she went on and on about how Tolani should have been on the pill or at the very least used a condom and how irresponsible she was to get *herself* in this position. And she *knows* that sex is enjoyable, but it also comes with serious conditions.

Tolani laughed when she said 'enjoyable.' Apparently, this was funny.

She sat through all of this, *whilst I was out playing football.*

But you know, shit happens.

The baby was gone.

I asked no questions and we carried on as usual.

Until that time I left my phone around her, and of course, she looked through it.

I tried to switch it up on her, I did the whole 'why you looking through my phone?' speech.

I mean *yes*, I was texting other girls, but that's *my phone* and *my privacy!* How dare she look through it, she doesn't pay my bills.

But she didn't buy that *this* time.

She just screamed and carried on screaming. 'How can you do this to me?' 'How can you do this to me NOW?' 'After everything, how can you do this to me again.' After I bought to the cutest little baby gloves from that shop on the high street. That shop that doesn't accept returns, but were happy for me to exchange the gloves for any other items. But all the other items are for babies and what good will that be, without a baby. After I skipped the enjoyable part of sex the nurse spoke about and went straight to the serious conditions bit.

She said she didn't want to be here any more. And not that she wanted to die – she just didn't want to live this life anymore. And how she couldn't believe that she was crying whilst I was out offering out subsided dick.

Dick that did nothing for anyone, EVER!

Dick that came with *so* many shortcomings.

And then she started laughing, like really moving mad.

'You really are a piece of shit. You had the cheek, the actual audacity to swing your stick back and forth like it's some sort of magic. To give other women the same below standard dick you give me. How shameless of you, to pass that around when I'm out here having 'orgasms' to soothe your ego. When sex with you is rarely pleasurable, just lonely. When my fake moans act as a trophy for your performance, cause they sure as hell weren't from pleasure!'

It was mad, she was crying but also laughing. So I grabbed her. I tried to hold her close to tame her anger. Because that's what happens in all them dumb films she watches. But that doesn't work in real life, because she fought her way out. And she just kept fighting.

So I replied…

'Well, the other girls ain't complaining.'

And then she just went silent.

You know that silence that precedes the storm? But rather than it feeling like the worst was over, I knew this was just the beginning.

She stopped laughing and wiped the tears from her face.

She asked if I had made the other girls feel the way she felt.

She asked if they had sat alone in a waiting room, crying.

If they too had to stay awake whilst life literally got taken out of them. Because that's what happens when you go alone, you have to stay awake.

She asked if the other girls were haunted by the memory of entering a white room, removing their clothes and folding them into a neat little pile on the side. Or if the other *lucky girls* were haunted by Alesha Dixon's 'Breathe Slow' because it was the only song playing in the waiting room.

And, if after going through the most traumatic experience of their life, their first thought was to go get me chicken and chips, because I would be hungry after *football.*

She asked if they would have wrapped the chicken and chips box with a scarf so it didn't get cold and if they too would have laughed at my shit joke about the chicken getting bird flu.

Or did they skip all of that and just get the 'enjoyable' bit of sex with me?

Pause, just a little too long. It's uncomfortable.

You see that was the thing with Tolani, she never really told me how much I hurt her. She cried, my God did she cry, but she never really said how broken she was.

She never even said those words to me.

But I felt it in her silence. I knew she wanted to pass her pain on to me. She wanted me to want to scream every time I heard the country acoustic strumming of...

'You're still the one...'

She didn't want to be hopeful with me any more, she didn't want to be with me anymore. The dream was dead.

And yeah it's sad, but that's just our story. It's not rhythmic or melodic. It's not what it was supposed to be.

Tolani Shoneye, aka Tolly T, is podcaster and writer. She is one of the hosts and producer of The Receipts Podcast, an award-winning sex and relationships podcast. Outside of this, Tolani has established herself as a writer and journalist. Her journalism work has seen her write for *BuzzFeed, Elle, The Independent* and *Refinery 29*; as a writer, she has penned the trailer for Netflix's *TopBoy*, and has a monologue platform called *Story Story*, where she explores her love for storytelling.

NOTE: Before we start, a little warning to whoever is reading this. There are words in this letter that may beguile your tongue. Parts of it will probably sound like shit. That's fine. Don't fight it. Good luck.

Living in Singapore, I didn't grow up with white people. But I do have a white best friend, and have ever since I was born. I suspect many of you do too. Have the same white best friend, that is. She has a way of lurking around the inner corners of the mouths of people the world over. Like syphilis. Through tongue to tongue contact.

My white best friend goes by many names. Lengua. Langue. She tou. Tongue. My colonized tongue. She reaches back, deep, into my throat like a massive Roman road, slowly peters away into pathways of veins, a glittering cartography of nerves, then synapses, into the colonized part of my brain, the language centre, full of its colonized neurons. My language centre.

This letter is written to you, about you, in you, by you, my white best friend, as everything today seems to be.

My dear tongue,

We've had good times. Haven't we? Let me list the top ten most recent.

1. Let's get this one out of the way. 'You speak amazing English for a' blank. Audience, take a moment to insert yourself in blank.

2. Thanks for number one, sis, I owe you. Thanks for the reply, which is always 'thank you'. I never hesitate to say 'thank you'. Thank you also for the words to clap back, 'Singapore's a former British colony. English is our first language.' It never fails to gall me, how actually violent and fucked up the reality of that historical fact is. But every time I say it, all I get is a simple apology back, the same sort of apology you get if someone were to accidentally brush against your arm on the Tube.

When, really, the fact of the matter is more like they swooped into your mom's house with a nautical SWAT team, got her to sign the house over with some dodgy contracts, stole a bunch of her jewelry, dug up the garden, filled it with concrete, tore down the house, got your mom to serve tea, threw your mom out, built a multi-million-pound retail complex over the property, and then got your mom to work as the janitor for far below minimum wage. Sorry mate.

That's how simply we accept the fact that so much of the world's tongues are colonized by this fact, variations of this fact.

But back to the good times.

3. Moving to the UK is when you really showed me the perks of our best-friendship. The radical facility that you give me. How I code switch into the colonized places of the earth like

I'm a walking password to a giant Netflix account. How I can sit in the grotty smoking point of a stinking warehouse rave in Tottenham Hale and really feel the promises of the great global project made manifest. It's not all you, though, it's also the MDMA.

4. Mostly, moving to the UK, it's you that made me feel special. I don't sound like I look. And what's that? Chinese. But I'm *not* Chinese from the *mainland*. *Not* one of those head-to-toe Gucci types, stumbling over unfamiliar consonants, but sounding like a million bucks, a million dirty Chinese bucks, grotesque, vulgar, nouveau riche. A new way for people to hate us, to hate me. But speaking the way I do, see the relief at the butcher's when I buy my pork chops, as he observes you, my tongue, flapping about with the ease of a Chinese acrobat. I don't sound quite as chinky. Thanks for that.

5. 'You're not that bad,' says the white boy whose face I've been sucking for the past hour at some shitty club in Vauxhall. 'You're not that bad,' he says, 'you're not like other Chinese people. I really hate Chinese people.' I say, thank you?

6. Coming to the UK, they put the both of us, you and me, to the test. Specifically the IELTS (I-E-L-T-S), the International English Language Testing System. A two-hundred-pound test to make sure I speak the language. You really came through for me. I told the white British lady examiner as much, the examiner conducting the one-on-one speaking test. We were meant to be discussing 'Tell me about a time when you received good service,' and it somehow ended up with me saying '…and that's why I'm doing this test, to go to the UK to get a Master's degree in writing plays in this language that I'm *actually* perfectly fluent in.'

7. Got full marks, didn't I? The full White-British Embarrassment marks. When I arrive for registration at uni a couple of months later, the white registration lady looks at my language test scores and goes, 'Oh wow these are very high scores, congratulations.' I say, thank you?

Pause.

8. Thank you for the words. Some of my favourite, that roll of the tongue. 'Trippingly off the tongue,' as Hamlet says (8.5, thank you for *Hamlet* I guess?).

Optometrist
Perspicacious
Eloquent
Loquacious
Disambiguate
Arboreal
Chintz
Intimation

Audience, especially the colonized ones amongst us, take a moment to think of your favourite words.

Make an incantation of them.

I glide through the world on a seawind of poetry. What a gift, the way I give shape to my reality with this language. Like pearls, rolling out of my mouth. I never hoard them, they keep rolling up from the gullet. I open my mouth, and let you, my white best friend, spill, spill, out. Let the world hear. This precious currency of phonemes. I love the sound, how they clang, and sparkle, pitter patter, over the ground.

9. Thank you. For tricking me into listening to the hidden meanings of things. When the USA says 'we the people,' when the UK says, 'we the people,' I find myself interpellated (another good word), into that world. I slide comfortably into a strange bath of belonging. I'm not from here. I need to keep saying. I'm not from here. Stop talking to me, stop *talking* to me. I can hear you. I understand you.

10. I'm seven years old. My mother is ironing clothes. I'm playing at her feet. I say to her, 'I don't want to be Chinese.'

'But you are Chinese.'

'No. I speak English. I'm English.'

.

My tongue.

You sit in my mouth like a rock of salt, perhaps Cornish, from the taste of it.

You release into my mind flavours of ancient woodland. Chalky cliffs. Britannic seas. Haunted forests. Mountainous caves. Celtic stone. Bear fur coats. Oak. Cedar. Forest badgers, hedge hog. Stone path. Holloway.

An incantation of British geography, that thanks to you, I've found magical all my life, even before I saw any of these things.

You sit in my mouth and fill my brain with images of your ancient beginnings.

'Darkly falls the ancient wood of Windsor in the faerie gloaming.'

.

My tongue.

I'm writing this letter to you from Singapore. I'm back on holiday. Since moving to the UK, every time I come back here, I find the landscape more and more haunting. It's things like the trees. The trees on this island are truly magnificent, tangled, dark-haired, whorling, towering things, growing with an impossible tropical thickness.

When you first came to this island, the tropics, the heat, the hot places of the earth, you described it as a heart of darkness and mystery. And this is how I know, my tongue, that soon you will be inadequate to the task of describing my life.

You don't have a way to describe the heat of my country. *Scorching*, you might say, or, blandly, *hot*. But neither captures the sense of how it handles me like a rough lover fucking me hard from behind, the sadistic pleasure of it, of burning chili heat, how the sun bastes me with a slick of spicy honey, saps me, then bathes me in a membrane of humidity.

This is life-giving heat. Not *scorching*, which burns, but a heat that wills you to live, the kind of heat that urges a seed to grow, urges a tree to explode into an orgasm of grotesque tropical excess – flowers of the deepest fire, of the brightest incandescent red. You are inadequate to the task of living this landscape, this landscape that responds to the sun with the full spectrum of the world's colours. Colour so rich you have to refract the whiteness of light to see it.

You were okay, in the past, I guess, when the things that mattered were the things that mattered everywhere else, that you could find anywhere else. Words like:

Boarding gate
Interface
Gin & Tonic
Home page
Checkout

Now that I'm back home, I find myself standing before these ancient tropical trees, and sighing a lot. I linger, for a long time. Stand before a mangrove and long to be absorbed into it. I know that if I had the right incantation, I could just disappear, melt into the swamp.

But I don't. I don't know the ancient language of my home. I know the ancient incantations of the British countryside, but not for the mangrove river fifteen minutes from my parents' flat.

Because over two hundred years in Singapore, you've replaced the language of leisure for work, the language of paradise with capital, the language of confidence with whiteness. You've made the patois we speak, Singlish, sound like the uncouth squabbling of village idiots. You've taken the tropics and replaced it with a technocrat language of starched office clothes, air-conditioned science fiction techno-horror theme parks. The only resistance is the body's: hideous, absurd patches of sweat in the armpit of a salaryman's Oxford shirt.

*

My tongue, you've abused yourself into so many mouths. I think you forget you don't, you can't describe everything.

What you can't express, you steal. You take what's useful and make it your own, and soon we forget these were ever other tongues.

Here is an incantation of stolen words. Words that are scabbed-over wounds of conquest, words the linguistic equivalent of white girls Namaste-ing in mountainous Nepalese yoga retreats. Imagine this incantation in a swirl of italics to mark their otherness, curvy, at an angle, slanted, off:

Avatar
Karma
Swastika
Curry
Mango
Chintz
Dungaree
Pajama
Punch
Thug
Banana
Gorilla
Ketchup
Tea
Kowtow
Bamboo
Gingham
Taboo
Tattoo
Lute
Pariah
Loot.

My tongue, there are days I want to force you out of my mouth. But I know I cannot. Because you're my best friend. What the hell would I do without you?

The best I can do is bend you into other shapes, other tongues. Tongues that my body has inherited, but left unexercised. Tongues that will sound like shit in the mouth of whoever is reading this. Tongues that I can only describe in English.

Cantonese is the sound
of my maternal grandmother's
flip flops slapping wetly
against the kitchen floor,
as she changes the damp cloth
sweating under the rice cooker,
scoops steaming rice
slams it down over the table
to mark the start of dinner.

The language of describing flavours
too sweet too salty…
tai tim, tai ham
hou sek, hou mei, mm hou sek.
Always too much.
Sing song and street brawl.
My grandmother's tongue.
I do not speak it.

Malay, the ancient language of the seas that connect the fractured islands of my archipelago. The language of the land I love, I do not speak it. But it is the one that most often asks me – why not?

It is a rain of flowers, brightly hued and perfumed, it is warm wok fragrances, the names of trees and herbs, the sunny side of history, the one that gives Singlish its mischievous grin, but then turns around and in another aspect slow dances with oceanic melancholy.

It makes me miss the heat that radiates off the concrete, I want to press my cheek to it, kiss the ground, smell the air, spy on my parent's childhood, listen to the muttering of the island's ghosts, the island's mournful heartbeat.

This is the language the whole island once spoke.

Listen to this incantation, this displaced language, this colonised language, this language you wrapped yourself around and strangled in the womb, a song of grief sung to the sea:

Bunga lah tanjung hai putih berseri
Ditiup bayu bunga nya jatuh
Duduk terlengung seorang lah diri
Kekasih dirindu sayang nya jauh…

Joel Tan is a Singaporean playwright based in London. In Singapore, his plays have been produced by leading theatre companies like Checkpoint Theatre, Wild Rice, and Pangdemonium, and several are available in a collection, *Joel Tan Plays Volume 1*, published by Checkpoint Theatre. Recent work in the UK includes *Love in the Time of the Ancients*, shortlisted for the 2019 Papatango Prize, and *No Particular Order*, shortlisted for Theatre 503's 2018 Playwriting Award.

JACK THORNE

Dear Doctor, I forget your name, you worked in Swansea in 2001.

I'm sure you are a nice man. I'm sure you are incredibly hard-working. I'm sure this was just a bad day. I love the NHS. The NHS has been very good to me. I already feel guilty about writing this. Rachel De-Lahay made me.

But I was asked where the shadows lie, and the truth is, you cast the largest one.

Because you told me I wasn't going to get better.

And I needed some positivity, because I was wretched.

Positivity is already a word I regret.

But looking at it I can't seem to think of a better one.

I had a condition called cholinergic urticaria. I had chronic cholinergic urticaria. Try saying that quickly. The rich witch won a wrist watch, which watch did the rich witch win. Chronic cholinergic urticaria.

And do you know why I hide behind such a pretty convoluted name: because, in reality, what's hidden underneath is prickly heat.

I had prickly heat. You know that thing you sometimes get when you stay out in the sun too long? That's all I had. And it utterly ruined my life.

Because I had it – chronically. I was allergic to the sun, I was allergic to radiators, I was allergic to any heat at all. I was slowly walking around in shorts and a T-shirt in Cambridge in December and I was still covered in spots. I became allergic to my own body movement, because every time you move you create heat. I was powerfully, painfully, allergic to heat.

Rick Edwards, he presents *Impossible* on BBC1, was at college with me, I was with him once when I was having a reaction, he asked me once to pull up my top and show me what the allergy looked like, and then told me it was disgusting and to pull my top down and never show it to anyone ever again. Rick Edwards is lovely btw, he actually is. And he's the first cool friend I ever had. Rachel De-Lahay, incidentally, is the second cool friend. She's a tastemaker.

But basically it looks like angry red spots. Like shingles if you've ever had them. I once achieved perfect shingles, where there was no space for any skin, I was just a pure red raw spot. Interestingly it also makes your muscles all look much more muscly. Your skin just sort of fills out. I don't know why it does that. I didn't look like the red hulk, I was a skinny runt, but I definitely looked more defined in allergy mode. Which it was nice to be a tourist in.

I'm getting off the point.

My condition got steadily worse. I went to doctors. They tried me on all sorts of medication. It kept deteriorating.

It got so bad I had to leave University. I couldn't be near any heat, then I couldn't be near any people, and then I couldn't move.

Cambridge University, where I was, handles this really nicely. If you want to leave Cambridge with illness, you have to ask to be degraded. So I degraded myself in front of them and then I went home.

To live with my parents again.

In Wales, where I'd never lived before.

The year I'd gone to University my Dad had retired and bought a dilapidated house in Tenby. He was having a weird time too. He'd worked in local government and had been passed over for promotion again and so had taken early retirement in his mid fifties and moved back to the place he was born. He'd decided he was going to set up his own business, he was going to make Pembrokeshire pasties cool again. You've heard of Cornish pasties right? Well, apparently there was a tradition of Pembrokeshire pasties at one point. He then tried to make pasties cheap enough to make some profit on them, and basically he couldn't do it without just making them out of mashed potato and swede (which doesn't taste that nice, believe me we had to eat a lot of them) and so he was now working out what he'd do instead. He was on the bottom floor, depressed, with my mum. I was on the top floor. With all the windows open. In bed. Depressed.

My parents didn't visit me much in my room, it was freezing. My Mum did however make me a lot of food to eat. A cake a week. She loved and loves me very much. But the trouble with not moving and eating a lot is you quickly accumulate some fat. I put on seven stone. Very quickly actually. Remarkably quickly. And changing size from eleven stone, which I was, to eighteen stone, is – well, quite a size difference.

So I was in pain, I was fat, I was unhappy, I was depressed.

By the way for all those writers who seek pain in order to write better – and I know you're out there – I remember a friend of mine being broken up with by a sci-fi novelist 'because she made him too happy' – you don't really write better when you're in pain. At least in my experience. I kept a journal and I kept writing plays, and everything I wrote during that time is horseshit. Utter horseshit. Why? Turns out self-pity is not attractive.

Is this letter still full of that self pity? Abso-fucking-lutely.

I can still access it.

Rather too easily.

Anyway, obviously, I had to keep visiting doctors and hospitals. Mostly we'd just go to the local village hospital when the reactions got too bad, and they'd just chuck me full of anti-histamine and wait for me to de-redden. But sometimes I'd go to the bigger hospital in Swansea to visit consultants, which meant a very, very painful drive and a very, very painful wait in a generally over-heated waiting room – it is so weird being aware of the heat in every room you walk into – even now, I gave up the last of my medication a year ago and am mostly free of the urticaria, but even now I do a heat assessment in every room I walk into. My dad drove me, we talked about pasties mostly. Actually, one time he had to drive me back to Cambridge for treatment – an almost eight-hour drive in a cold cold car – respect to you, Dad – but then we mainly listened to the radio.

It's in the Swansea hospital we met you.

Now skin doctors – dermatologists if you will – come in all shapes and sizes. It's a very broad church I think dermatology and it's not one that seems to get a lot of support. When I was going regularly to hospital, dermatology clinics tended to be on one or two days a week. Heart doctors are there all the time, dermatologists have to keep moving around – nomads constantly looking for a place and a home where they are respected. Littlest hobos all. This is all just supposition, I've never talked to a dermatologist outside of surgery, but I bet they feel a tiny bit unloved generally.

You definitely felt unloved that day.

You were in a bad mood with me from the start.

And I did that thing, because by this point I'd had the condition for nine months, and for three months it'd kept me in my bed, of sounding a bit like I understood it. Which must be fucking annoying. I remember a friend of mine coming back in tears from a GP because the GP had refused to prescribe her drugs, my friend was a medical student and had her diagnosis ready for the GP, the GP hadn't taken it well. I suspect I was a bit like that to you. Which is a dickish thing to be when you need help. And I did need help from you.

But I don't know, honestly, how many patients you'd had like me. In Cambridge I'd been meeting some really cool specialists who were – and I don't think this is the wrong word to use – fascinated by me. At one point it had been suggested that I might need to be presented at a conference with all the doctors saying their piece about me – but then I'd degraded and that idea had gone away. You weren't fascinated. You were just irritated. Or maybe out of your depth. It's a weird illness to have as chronically as I did and most doctors when they talked to me, had to look some things up, had to check through books, to understand the medication I was on, had to ask questions about what had been tried before, what my treatments were. You didn't do any of that. Maybe you had a long list that day. I don't know.

I told you the drugs seemed to be working. I was on sixteen pills a day then – four little pink pills twice a day that were anti-anxiety and anti-histamine, four little white pills twice a day that were mast cell stabilisers (mast cells are part of your immune system), and two big anti-histamine anti-depressants before sleep. I told you that the allergic reactions were still there and still crippling, but they weren't quite as severe as they had been. I told you I still wasn't able to move much though. I asked whether I was on a healing curve. I asked when you thought I might be able to start going downstairs more, when I might get out of bed.

You turned to me – you looked me in the eye – just the one – in both my eyes and said – you've been on the pills three months now, you have tried every other kind of medication with little effect, these pills are having an effect, they are probably the right ones, the chances are this is as good as it's going to get, this is probably going to be how it is for the rest of your life.

Now, there are a lot of people who've heard the same thing. I've worked quite extensively in the disabled world now, a more positive letter I could have written for this thing is to Alex Bulmer, a very excellent blind woman who told me I was not only welcome at a Graeae open day but that I belonged there, that I was a disabled person. That label felt very important, like

I was coming out, like I had a community that understood me and understood what constant pain felt like.

There are a lot of people who've heard the same thing, that cope with it bravely, people that are amazing, but it wasn't something I needed to hear. It wasn't something that was good for me to hear.

Maybe it the was right diagnosis, maybe I shouldn't have got better, maybe this was something I needed to see as a long-term thing, but I was so miserable that the idea of this stretching on and on – the idea of not being able to turn off the pain… I don't know… The month or so after I left you was hell. It had been hard before, but that feeling of this is it, this is forever – I couldn't shake it off. I had severe and constant suicidal thoughts, I even set deadlines in my head. I knew I couldn't continue…

But I did – continue – and it turns out, you were wrong. I did get better and I think it was despite of you, not because of you. I think it was through the miracle of medication and the kindness of other doctors. It took me about four months to be fully out of bed, it took me five years or so to be comfortable enough in daily life, ten years for it not to be a constant concern, and eighteen years to give up my medication. I lost some of the weight, using the cereal diet – two bowls of cereal a day, one meal, yay. I went back to University at the start of the next academic year and survived, albeit with a 2.2, albeit with going to hospital twice a week for this strange treatment where I had to stand in a heat shower, but it was okay. I still have bouts of illness where the urticaria comes back. The last time about a month ago. But it's generally left me alone.

I don't know, Doctor, this letter has left me confused. Maybe the Norman Tebbit of 'this is all down to you now, get on your bike, get well' – maybe that was good for me. The spurn I needed. I fucking hate Norman Tebbit but maybe I did try harder. Maybe that's why I remember you so well.

But I don't think that's right.

I suppose there are two sorts of people in the world. Those that need a kick and those that need a hand. Those that vote Conservative and believe in self-help, and those that vote Labour and believe in support. Even amongst writers I know the same is true. I worked on a TV show called *Skins* and another writer on that show told me that he needed people to think he wasn't capable of something, he needed to be able to prove them wrong. I've always thought of myself as someone who needs a hand. I've always preferred the people that give me the hand, not the kick. I am arrogant enough to write, but not confident in any other way; I avoid people and parties and life generally, and people who know me know this. When Rachel De-Lahay told me this was gig theatre, I said 'how exciting, I won't come' and she said 'of course not'. I need support, and I hope – hope – I recognise I need to support others in order to get it back. That's the world I want to live in. That's the people I want to spend time with.

You are – were, perhaps you're dead or perhaps you've changed – not one of those people. In fact, you remain the least supportive person I've ever met in my life. And I've worked in television, with a lot of very angry producers.

So instinctively I'm still angry with you for what you said. Instinctively I think you should have done better than deny hope to someone clearly on his knees. Instinctively I feel like I teetered on the brink of total destruction and that the outcome of what you said could have been suicide, could have been it. And that's why I wrote this letter. I think.

Jesus, this was much harder than I expected.

Gig bloody theatre.

Jack Thorne is a playwright and screenwriter. Recent plays include *the end of history...* (Royal Court Theatre, 2019), *A Christmas Carol* (Old Vic, 2017), *Woyzeck* (Old Vic, 2017), *Junkyard* (Headlong/Bristol Old Vic/Rose Theatre Kingston/Theatr Clwyd, 2017) and *Harry Potter and the Cursed Child* (Palace Theatre, 2016. He was a core writer in all three series of *Skins* (E4, Channel 4); other TV writing includes *This Is England '86*, *This Is England '88*, and *This Is England '90*.

NOTE: Dear Mr Artistic Director, please know I did my research for this. Now stand centre stage and hold your dick throughout!

Hi. I used to run a major new writing theatre, in one of the most exciting cities in the world, and once looked into the eyes of a young writer and promised them a commission to write an entirely new play. They smiled – gratefully explaining that the money from that would come in very useful.

I never called her again. Who am I?

Hi. I once called in a theatre practitioner to ask all about their background – culturally and financially – in the promise of a job as a collaborator on an exciting new project. After all thoughts had been shared, the exciting new project went ahead – without that curator's involvement. In any capacity. Who am I?

I offer diverse practitioners employment in outreach programs so the people they are reaching out to can see themselves reflected in theatre as an example of who they can be…

An outreach practitioner.

They are not invited to take up actual space in the theatre. Who am I?

I curate unpaid 'diversity panels' to discuss change and progress, but never once follow them up with the offer for those involved to make work here. Who am I?

I talk lots about work that reflects the make-up of our city. 'London must be reflected on our stages,' I say. However, everyone I employ – apart from a few members of bar staff – is white. Who am I?

I sat across from a practitioner in a meeting and, pondering as to whether or not they were suitable for a job – that I held the keys for – asked her to describe to me the day they lost their virginity. That question had nothing to do with the job. I was just curious. Who am I?

I rubbed my dick against an actress in a toilet once. I say once. It was the only time anyone complained. Who am I?

I took an actor who'd graced my stage to my South London abode. We did all the mara-ju-warna and ALL of the cocaine whilst I talked him though my homoerotic fantasies. He informed me he was straight. I leapt anyhow.

He ran. I blocked him. Who am I?

I slid into the DMs of a twenty-five-year-old who was talking to me merrily – some might say flirtily – in the smoking area of the *Evening Standard* Awards, offering to 'put her to bed properly.' Who am I?

I sent a picture of my dick. My actual dick.

Maybe. The receiver could never prove anything 'cause she blocked me – I assume turning down any opportunity to compare the two images in real life. Who am I?

When a theatre practitioner was the target of a lewd sexual remark and went on to tell me what happened, I said that she needed to get over it. Who am I?

I talk a lot about how nothing will change unless we see more diversity across leadership roles. But I won't be giving up my leadership role.

I felt passionate about a BAME theatre company and so decided to run it, even though I am not BAME. Some people complained. Luckily I didn't lose my job 'cause white men don't lose. Who am I?

I say I like to be challenged, but won't call you again if you do.

I don't check my emails. Ever. Like never. Like if you want to get ahold of me it'll be impossible. I'm so busy. Just frightfully busy. After you hand in your script, that I badgered you for, you will never see nor hear from me again. You might try and be smart and rock up at theatres for previews of shows I'm directing, knowing for a fact I'll be there, but that's where my true skill shines the brightest. I smile wide –

Wider –

And bamboozle you with such an energy you'll forget why you were even approaching me, before quickly reminding you of my busyness and running away.

In the unlikely event you act bolder than any of us could imagine – and ask 'if I've read your script?' I'll give you a look –

Like a head tilt and a slanted smile that says – 'how are you being this brave? How are you not just assuming it's a no? Why would you not *think* it's a no?

With how many commissions we give out, and how many productions we put on – the odds are it *is* a no.

And yet here you are…being brave.

And no I haven't even read it. 'Cause of all the busy! But you should be being *quiet* and *coy* and *nervously anxious assuming* it's a no!

So I can get back to all of that busy. 'Cause if it wasn't a *no* before this, it sure as hell is a no *now!*'

I do all that with a smile. I find the smile really easy. They teach you at gatekeeper school. Who am I?

Other things they teach you at gatekeeper school…

Talk loudly about diversity. Say LOUDLY we want more women making theatre – all women – queer women, black-brown women –

(Say that bit quickly 'cause truly what is the difference? And like your aunt Jemima once said – aren't we all black? Deep down? Like – don't we all come from Africa?)

Black-brown women, green women! We want the green women the most! Where are all the green women?

And when anyone ever questions the fact that including *women* isn't being diverse, smile wide –

Wider –

And say quite simply – 'Well that's the problem isn't it? Angry mediocre practitioner – who no one wanted to the employ anyhow –'

(Lesson number two at gatekeeper school bleeds into number one and that's the ability to recognise those that shout the loudest are the ones with the least talent.

Like of course you can see we somehow got away with having not one female writer/director for nearly an entire year –

'cause you are *bored* and have nothing else to fill your day with.)

(They really are rarely talented foghorns, which is useful for when they make exceedingly good points – to just dismiss them as such.)

With that and – 'I don't see colour.'

'I'd rather curate my season based on talent. Actually. Instead of having a disabled director for the sake of it. Like maybe I don't like the one disabled director that I know's direction?

Is that not okay? Am I not allowed to have taste?

And if my building isn't even accessible to them anyway, and I have no plans to spend any of my budget making my building accessible, isn't this all a moot point.'

Also learn (after spending the first term not learning what diverse even means) a really deep understanding that there just isn't that much diversity out there. 'I've yet to even truly meet a diverse practitioner worthy of a job over a white. Maybe Lin Manuel. Or Idris. I'd take an Idris. If he's written by a white.

And whilst we're on the subject – remind them that we're not allowed a white Othello. So…

Shrug.

And if that's not anti-colourblind casting I don't know what is.

And in truth…

There is just no way we could find an eclectic mix of voices and styles – over twenty writers from completely different worlds – to put on an entirely new festival of new writing that's sold out every day. There's no way we could do that. And even if we did, it would never get the support of mainstream press – no one would come and review it – no decent actors would support it…

And also, what if we did – what if we took that risk and made that night and it all failed – loudly – disastrously – then what? Black and brown and queer voices failing –

Not entertaining – no one caring – people leaving unsatisfied – what then?

Sure we put on ▓▓▓▓▓▓▓ but…

But *they* can't fail so…

It would be too much of a hindrance to the movement. So let's not even try. And instead put on another ▓▓▓▓▓ favourite adapted by ▓▓▓▓▓▓▓▓▓.'

I am the head of an Arts Council-run theatre in the UK funded by your money.

My job is to source the talent and produce their productions in said buildings for your entertainment – not you bratty theatre peeps whose mummies and daddies got you jobs here and have never paid for a goddam ticket in your life – this *ish* ain't for you! But the paying public up and down the country – of varying backgrounds and experiences. *You.*

What *defines* 'talent' is entirely up to me.

I can put on anything I choose – absolutely anything.

You may be naive and assume I am answerable to some money people or some such, but as an Artistic Director and Chief Executive at the same time, which is what most of the structure is in Britain for theatre, basically financially and artistically the buck stops with me. Sure, I have an amazing team of very senior people who are there to advise, but ultimately it's my decision.

And how do I use that power…?

> *Let go of your dick. It's gross.*

Hi. My name is Chris Sonnex and this all isn't me – hasn't been me – I hope – don't think – though if you disagree – I'm here and will be here to listen and hear and learn 'cause it could be – bits, small bits, entire bits. I'm here.

My name is Chris Sonnex and I recently got appointed a job – a powerful job – in a central London building. This building. I then text my friend –

We became friends through work 'cause in that space she was one of the few people who looked like me, was raised like me, and obsessed about Air Max like me. We clung to each other. I even introduced her to my best friend, Jerome.

She assumed I said *Tyrone* and though that was fucking rude, I knew it wasn't laziness, but because she knows many a Jerome *and* Tyrone and that was a fucking mistake!

(This is her *still* not apologizing!)

I then sent her a text asking if we could run a festival. In my new space with a director I adored who she'd worked with a lot. I guess this is an example of nepotism. But until the system is fixed – bun the system!

My name is Chris Sonnex and ultimately I am here – in a new capacity – having the *real* mistakes of the past laid out bluntly at my feet. And being asked to do better.

Thank *you* for this opportunity.

Now let me get back to bloodclart work!